Nurse for the Moment

By

Julia D. Stevens, RN, MSN

ISBN: 1-4033-0069-0 (Softcover)
ISBN: 1-4033-0068-2 (Electronic)

Library of Congress Control Number: 2002101134

This book is printed on acid free paper.

Printed in the United States of America
Bloomington, IN

1stBooks - rev. 05/22/02

ACKNOWLEDGMENTS

The author has been extremely grateful for the time, effort and expertise during the past several years of the following nurses for their helpful advice and encouragement in the completion of this narrative journal:

Leslie H. Nicoll, PhD, MBA, R.N.

Katherine A. Meyer, R.N., D.N.S.

ABOUT THE BOOK

"Nurse for the Moment" is a compilation of my observations and reflections during two years of assignments as an independent nurse contractor visiting more than 1,027 patient-families in the greater metropolitan Boston and Lowell regions. "Nurse for the Moment" is a narrative journal, tape-recorded at the close of the day's work, and later transcribed. In this journal format, I have described the role and responsibilities of the independent nurse contractor, the diversity of patient-families, their complex medical and social problems, and the impact of environmental conditions and patients' health insurance status on the nurse's performance.

I have also sought to describe the depth of knowledge, experience, and confidence which are necessary to provide accurate assessments, treatment, instruction and evaluation of patients on a single visit basis. There are numerous in-depth descriptions of clinical interventions with patient-families which could serve as exemplars for community health nurses.

I believe my story is one of great relevance and importance to health policy experts, to administrators of home health agencies, to nurse faculties of schools of nursing and to nurses who are considering the new and challenging field of independent contracting.

TABLE OF CONTENTS

INTRODUCTION

After being employed for many years in various health care institutions, I realized that I now wanted to be more independent. I wanted to remain in community health nursing, but in a position that would allow me flexibility of working hours and days, the opportunity to again feel the gratification of clinical patient-family care and to be in control of the quality of care given. I also thought that this type of position would afford me the chance to observe the dynamic forces both within and without community health nursing agencies which influence the quality of staff nurses' and per diem contractors' work.

The concept of independent contracting by community health nurses is a new phenomenon in our society. It is reflective of current trends, as more nurses with higher education, years of experience, and certification as specialists seek the autonomy and freedom to set their own working pace which self-employment can afford them. In reading "Future Shock", I found that Alvin Toffler (1970) expressed my current viewpoint with exactitude. He quoted Warren Bennis, the renowned social psychologist, as saying that professional specialists "seemingly derive their rewards from inward standards of excellence, from their professional societies, and from the intrinsic satisfaction of their task. In fact, they are committed to the task, not the job; to their standards, not their boss. And because they have degrees, they travel. They are not good 'company men'; they are uncommitted except to the challenging environments where they can 'play with problems'." (p. 148)

An independent nurse contractor is a registered professional nurse with many years of community health experience. She/he contracts with an agent to perform home health nursing visits to patients who are receiving services from a certified community health nursing (usually a visiting nurse) agency. Independent contractor status is assured under Internal Revenue Service regulations because the independent nurse contractor sets her/his own hours of work, performs without direct supervision, accepts assignments in more than one agency and is paid on a per visit basis by a third party rather than by the visiting nurse agency. The independent contractor is responsible for payment of all taxes, social security, and expenses (some of which are tax-deductible). No benefits are paid by the agent to the nurse contractor. Independent contractors provide their own essential nursing assessment equipment, such as a stethescope and sphygmomanometer.

As an independent contractor, I utilized Community Health Network, Inc. (CHNI) of Cambridge, Ma. as an assignment and compensation agent, contracting on a per diem basis to provide comprehensive nursing care in the home setting. CHNI is a for-profit organization "created to provide experienced community health nurses with per diem work at community health agencies. It provides agencies with access to a pool of experienced professional community health nurses to accomodate fluctuating needs for staff." (CHNI, 11/89) I agreed to accept assignments at one regional suburban agency, one urban agency, one small city agency and one regional urban/suburban agency, for these four agencies were all within twenty miles of my home. Upon arrival at a designated visiting nurse agency, I would then negotiate with the supervisor for the number of patient-visits to be made each day.

Criteria for Professional Nursing Visits

I would be expected to be accountable for high quality patient care and a level of charting which would demonstrate medical necessity and skilled nursing intervention, to utilize the nursing process of assessment, plan, intervention and evaluation in delivery of care, and to communicate (via submitted documentation) to the area supervisor all information related to patient visits upon completion of work.

Patient-Visit Guidelines

The patient-visit guidelines included the following criteria:
documenting each visit to reflect medical necessity and skilled nursing care, completing and signing the flow chart, writing narrative notes in SOAP format (Subjective Complaint, Nurse's Observation, Nurse's Assessment & Diagnosis, Plan of Action), telephoning MD for clarification of orders or change of orders when indicated, writing speed memos for phone call follow up, ordering supplies (dressings, catheters, DME, O2, etc.), updating medication list and problem list, home health aide introductions/ supervisions, changing fees and completing necessary forms, and writing discharge summaries. An admission visit requires that the Form 485 (Health Care Finance Administration HCFA) be completed in addition to the data base, problem list, care plan, medication sheet, authorization for care, and any other forms pertinent to the particular agency's protocols. (CHNI Requirements, 11/89)

Thus, extensive experience in community health documentation is an essential requirement of independent contractors, who work without direct supervision and usually see each patient only once. The contractors must be absolutely certain that their documentation of each patient's care coincides with the primary nurse's nursing care plan, so that the outcome will be reimbursable under health insurors' guidelines. When conducting an admission, the contractor's documentation must also conform to the agency's unique record-keeping system and meet the requirements of the Department of Public Health as well.

I want to emphasize that throughout this journal, I have used fictitious patient names, agency titles, and town identities in order to protect family privacy and agencies' reputation from possible public criticism.

PREFACE

NURSE FOR THE MOMENT

This book is a narrative journal of my personal thoughts, concerns, observations and reflections during the two years I spent as an independent nurse contractor providing in-home intermittent nursing care to 1,027 patient-families throughout the area of metropolitan Boston, Massachusetts.

I had previously been employed for several years as a community health (primary) staff nurse in several visiting nurse agencies, and had most recently served as administrator/supervisor for a combined town public health and community health nursing agency.

When I decided to undertake this type of temporary or per diem nursing work, I wanted to document my experiences. (I also had a great yen to write, but no time or energy to sit down with a word processor after working all day.)

I purchased a tape recording machine to dictate descriptions of my day's work which would provide accurate and factual information as I experienced it and which could be transcribed at a later time. Much to my surprise, I discovered that dictating into my small machine relieved my pent-up stress and fatigue, as well as affording me the means of validating my nursing work and the concerns I had had as a direct care provider to many very ill and frail patients.

Very few nurses take the time to validate their work. They have been carefully taught never to talk about their patients beyond the confines of the work-place, in order to protect patients' confidentiality as well as the intimate and personal nature of nurses' work. Thus all of their concerns, doubts, decisions, actions, accomplishments and defeats regarding their patients never are validated, either verbally or in writing.

I had never seen in print a truly factual account over an extended period of time of the actual working conditions of today's community health nurse. I thought it might be a story worth telling, particularly as health insurors' emphasis was now on early hospital discharge with limited home health care coverage for millions of patients. It would provide an opportunity to tell about the benefits of home health nursing care, the problems in providing high quality and continuity of care, the differences between traditional community health nursing and today's home health care nursing, and the need for both nurse and patient-family satisfaction in delivery of care.

The examples described in this journal illustrate some of the differences between large and small community nursing agencies—their organizational and administrative structure, record-keeping, staff and contract nurses' abilities, level of morale and turn-over rate, patient-family satisfaction, and other variables which affect nurses' satisfaction and quality of care given. I was also able to compare and contrast my first year of contracting experience with the second year, and to describe how my experiences affected my impressions and performance from one year to the next.

Other examples described in this journal should be helpful to those nurses who are considering independent contractor work as well as to administrators of visiting nurse agencies who may be able to affect positive changes to promote improved quality of patient care and nurse satisfaction. The many clinical descriptions of patient-families and utilization of the nursing process may serve as examplars for nursing students in baccalaureate nursing programs. Lastly, it is my hope that nurses who happen to read this journal will decide to validate their own nursing experiences. Eventually then, a large number of narrative journals will be available for nurse researchers to draw upon as qualitative data to improve the art and science of nursing, as well as its value to society.

THE SETTING

Visiting nurse agencies have been prevalent in both large and small towns since the late 1800's. They are non-profit, voluntary organizations whose mission is to provide primary, secondary and tertiary health care to individuals, families and aggregate groups in each community. To quote Stanhope & Lancaster (1988), "The key difference between community health nursing and the other areas of nursing is the emphasis on the personal and environmental health of the total population, not just of selected individuals...It focuses on the physical, biological, social, psychological, and environmental health of a population group...community health nurses anticipate, estimate, and design measures to interrupt the onset of personal health problems...their focus is specific, highly complex, and scientific...It takes considerable skill to estimate the potential onset of a health problem as a result of unsafe living conditions and intervene before health problems ensue." (pp 24-25)

Today's community health nurses have been retitled as "primary" nurses. According to Zander (1985), primary nurses are registered nurses, not necessarily baccalaureate prepared, who are employed in hospitals and who are responsible for the outcomes of care for their patients. The high acuity of patients discharged to home health agencies for short-term highly technical nursing care has become associated with use of the term "primary nurse"; but in reality, community health nurses have always been responsible for the outcomes of long and short-term care of their patient-family case-loads.

Primary community health nurses are usually full-time staff employees and many are graduates of baccalaureate nursing programs; thus they have had several months' training in the field of community health, particularly practice in developing case management skills. According to Grau (1986) case management has historically been the largest part of the community health nurse's role. However, there is now less emphasis on case management as an essential component of the primary nurse's role in certified community health nursing agencies. As will be described later on in this journal, the emphasis on patient care is rapidly shifting from the health promotive, preventive care principles involved in case management to that of episodic care of the acutely ill, post-hospital patient. The primary nurse's focus and goal is to see how quickly she can help the patient to achieve health stability and discharge from services, even though other potential health problems of the patient and his family may not have been addressed.

Independent nurse contractors are registered nurses with extensive background experience in community health nursing. They have varied educational backgrounds;however, from the basic hospital-trained registered nurse to master's degree preparation in community health or another specialty. Most have at least a baccalaureate degree in nursing. Their function is to serve as per diem replacements for the primary nurse who may be absent due to illness, vacation, or a conference day. The contract nurse carries out the primary nurse's care plan, performing such task related skills as physical assessments, dressing changes, medication checks, and home health aide supervisions, but she/he does not normally become involved with resource referrals, trust-building or coordination of caregivers, for these case management responsibilities take much extra time in the office, as well as considerable back-ground knowledge of the patient-family and of community resources.

Visiting nurse agencies are very busy places of work. Nurses are constantly admitting, caring for and then discharging patients at a rapid pace. Many patients receive care services for no more than three weeks— just enough time for their wounds to heal, their conditions to stabilize, or to adjust to a new medication regime. There are still many patients; however, whose conditions are chronic, and whose families are having difficulty in coping with their long-term care needs. The case management skills of a primary nurse are essential to maintenance of these patients in their homes.

Over the past ten years, as hospitals have discharged "quicker and sicker" patients, primary nurses have been assigned larger and more complex case-loads. Concommitantly, health insurors and the Department of Public Health have required substantially more documentation of care. As a result, primary nurses frequently become overburdened, either becoming ill themselves or resigning abruptly. Thus visiting nurse agencies are beginning to rely more frequently on the per diem services of independent nurse contractors. Utilization of contract nurses places additional responsibilities on supervisors, and can undermine the morale of primary nurses, who have invested so much energy, thought and time in building a trusting relationship with their patients and designing effective care plans. On the other hand, contract nurses can relieve much stress in agencies when they are over-loaded with new admissions by caring for some of the primary nurses' patients, offering new suggestions for care of difficult patients, or providing respite for the primary nurse who needs to spend the day at her desk completing documentation. Increasingly; however, contract nurses are being utilized as primary nurses, for agencies are experiencing a shortage of nurses willing to assume the full-time duties of primary nurse with case management responsibilities.

This, then, was the background in which I began my work as an independent nurse contractor—an endeavor, which thanks to my journal, I shall never forget and which will have made a contribution to nursing and to society.

Julia D. Stevens, R.N.,C.S., MSN
April 15, 1995

PART I

SEPTEMBER 1991 TO JUNE 1992

Julia Stevens, RN, MSN

1. MY FIRST DAY AS AN INDEPENDENT CONTRACTOR

September 26, 1991: On this day, my birthday, I begin a new endeavor. I am feeling very independent, exhilarated, and slightly anxious as I drive twenty miles on a crowded commuter highway. In about 45 minutes I arrive at the offices of "Sunshine", a large suburban regional VNA, where I find an empty desk and am handed six patient records. In about an hour, I have telephoned each patient to set up an appointment time, studied my maps for contiguous driving patterns, ascertained the patients' diagnoses and plan of care for that day, and assembled the necessary nursing supplies. I have my own large waterproof nursing bag which contains the following equipment and supplies:

—a top of the line blood pressure cuff and stethescope, glucometer, measuring tape, bandage scissors, thermometers with covers, otiscope, flashlight, and drug reference book.
—agency supplied paper towels, liquid soap, hazard container, sterile and non-sterile gloves, tongue depressors, swabs, sterile specimen containers, suture kit, alcohol and betadine pads, sterile dressing supplies, tape, catheterization kit, extra sterile catheters, irrigation syringes, tuberculin, insulin and 2 cc sterile syringes.

My first patient, an elderly Portuguese gentleman, had recently been discharged from the hospital with a new diagnosis of diabetes mellitus complicated by a urinary tract infection, with foley catheter insertion. He and his wife spoke no English, but a son was willing and able to learn about the care of diabetes and translate the information to his parents. We were visiting this family twice a day, doing capillary glucometer readings to ascertain the patient's blood sugar levels, so that his insulin dosage could be adjusted appropriately. He was on a liquid diet, due to gastritis; and thus it was difficult to ensure balanced amounts of protein, fat and carbohydrates. I spent 45 minutes there, ascertaining the family's learning needs, and teaching use of glucometer and insulin syringes, suggesting appropriate liquids, skin care and need to sit up, deep breathe, and dangle every two hours to prevent pulmonary problems. The entire family was in a high state of stress for there had been many negative changes in a short time. The twice daily visits of visiting nurses were reassuring and helpful to them and allowed us time to reinforce diabetic teaching, answer questions, and assess for complications.

I then found my way along unfamiliar streets to the home of an elderly couple who lived in a small, second floor subsidized apartment. The man was very frail; he had many physical problems requiring total care by his devoted wife. It became obvious to me during the course of my assessment that he was beginning another urinary tract infection. I called his physician, who ordered a clean catch specimen. The patient's wife agreed to take the specimen to the physician's office promptly. Thus I instructed her in the mechanics of obtaining a clean catch, giving her a sterile container from the supplies in my bag. I felt great admiration for this woman's patience, strength and perseverence in caring for her husband with such dignity and kindness.

The fourth visit was to an elderly Italian lady who was confined to bed and chair following hip surgery. Mrs. Cellini had developed cellulitis in the opposite leg and a toe ulcer. I took care of her foot, re-bandaging it, assessing the cellulitis and evaluating the home health aide who was providing personal care and socialization. I was able to reassure them both that their care was appropriate and conducive to healing.

The last visit was to a 93 year old woman, a spinster, who lived alone, but who had daily housekeeping help. Miss Mary Gardner had very poor circulation in her legs but none the less had recently undergone a total knee replacement. Her feet were in poor condition; apparently no one had thought to bathe them while in the hospital, and she did not have a home health aide for personal care. I bathed both feet, applied Eucerin, and gave her a Vitamin B12 injection. I went over her medications and talked with her about the importance of arranging for daily foot and skin care. Mary was going to a life-care community the following week, as she realized that she needed total physical care. However, this delightful lady had a very independent and responsible outlook. I felt assured that she would remain in control of her life, no matter where she resided, and that she clearly understood the importance of daily foot and skin care. By then, it was around 1:30 PM; I headed back to the office, ate my sandwich lunch, and sat down to do my charting. I was tired, but relieved and satisfied with my first day's work as an independent contractor. I felt happy; I felt like a nurse again!

I was finally able to spend as much time as I felt necessary with each patient—no more rushing back to the office to do mountains of paper work. No more feelings of conflict with being unable to provide optimal nursing care due to the time constraints placed on primary nurse employees, who must hurry through their required number of daily visits in order to allow sufficient time back in the office for completing insurance documentation.

2. CITY CHALLENGES

October 3, 1991: I accepted assignment to an urban visiting nurse agency today, which I shall call "Riverside". The traffic going in on the commuter highway between 7 and 8 AM was extremely congested, but once there I was assigned five patients and thought I would have a good day. However, I misjudged the difficulty of negotiating the city streets and the lack of parking in front of people's homes. I finally did see five patients, several of whom were quite ill. The first was a newly diagnosed diabetic who spoke only Portuguese. Unfortunately, there was no one else at home who could serve as interpretor, so I was not able to communicate very effectively with her. I tested her blood glucose which was satisfactory; her vital signs were normal, and her skin and feet in good condition. Reassuring her that all was well I then moved on to another apartment building where an elderly man, a Portuguese and newly diagnosed diabetic, lived with his sister. They both could communicate sparingly in English. He had a right amputation below the knee that was infected. I changed his dressing, and then checked out his medications and cardio-pulmonary status. He was doing well, in part because his sister prepared nourishing Portuguese meals for him and reminded him to take his pills.

3. A DISCONCERTING VISIT

I then moved on to another part of the city. Unfortunately, the patient records did not include specific directions on how to get to many of the buildings. To my dismay, I discovered that there was no entrance to the large apartment building for the address given me. Eventually I found my way around to the rear of the building where the entrance was located and parking available. By this time, I was an hour late for my appointment which made me feel tense and anxious. (I soon learned not to agree to specific appointment times with patients, except when a home health aide supervision visit was due.) Another surprise was that the residents of this building were well-educated, older, upper middle class persons, a socio-economic group we visiting nurses rarely encounter. I felt disconcerted, for I realized that this group has many resources upon which to draw in time of illness, as well as a wealth of knowledge about physical health in general. I would have to alter my assessment and teaching techniques considerably to meet them effectively on their intellectual plane. The patient whom I saw, a lady of 94 years, was seated in a lovely book-lined living room filled with antique furniture. She was wearing a supportive collar around her neck. She had fallen and badly lacerated her lower left leg several weeks previously; she was unable to bend over to care for her wounds herself. As I changed her dressing and noted the very slow healing process, I began to talk with her about the importance of her diet. I assessed her dietary intake, which was deficient in protein and vitamins A, C and E. Apparently I had found a topic of interest to her; she responded positively to my teaching about the need to eat small amounts of protein-rich foods five to six times daily to promote more rapid healing. Together we created a short written list of nutritious snacks which her housekeeper could keep on hand. She thanked me profusely for my suggestions and I wished her "good health and more rapid healing".

The next patient was an elderly black woman who had moved from Washington a year ago to be near her family. Sarah Blodgett lived on the third floor of a subsidized housing apartment building and had severe cardiac disease. She also had metastasized colon cancer; there was a very hard mass in her abdomen. She had many vague aches and pains and difficulty moving about. Her cardiac status was very unstable. She had not been taking her nitroglycerine because she feared "she might explode." I explained the purpose, safety of, and effects of nitro to her and she agreed to take the nitro whenever she again had episodes of upper arm and chest pain and difficulty breathing. I then discovered that her electric hospital bed which had arrived with her from Washington had never been plugged in, so she was unable to elevate the head of her bed at night to relieve shortness of breath. I managed to plug in the bed and showed her how to operate it correctly and she agreed to use it. I reviewed all of her meds, placing her pills in separate envelopes because she had to take so many at varying times of the day. However, I wondered whether she would remember all that I had taught her, for she was so vague in her affect. I also re-ordered some of her prescriptions by telephoning the pharmacist. We discussed her diet and the difficulties she had in cooking, as she couldn't stand up long enough to prepare meals. I suggested frozen dinners, naming a well-known low sodium brand, and she wrote this suggestion down on her shopping list. Sarah was a lovely person and I really felt quite sorry for her in her lonely predicament of trying to cope with her terminal illness. I thought she needed a homemaker twice a week and a home health aide three days a week to assist her with household tasks, personal care and socialization. Possibly the admitting nurse had requested these services, but there were none available. Here was a patient who needed the on-going care and concern of a staff primary nurse, but for reasons unknown to me, one had not been assigned.

4. FEAR FOR MY SAFETY

My last visit was to still another Portuguese family who lived in one of those huge tall brick apartment buildings which were constructed with federal housing money in the early 1970's. Mrs. Maria Miguel lived up on the 17th floor; I stepped into an elevator crowded with all sorts of persons of unknown character. My anxiety was high, as I had heard about muggings and wondered what I should do if someone tried to grab my nursing bag. Maria lived with her daughter, who has AIDS, but really looked quite well, and she could speak English; fortunately, as could the home health aide. Maria was a stable diabetic whose skin was in excellent condition. I tend to feel somewhat superfluous in supervising home health aides in these long-term cases, for it is difficult to find any new areas for teaching, particularly as I don't know the family or the home health aide. This family had obviously already been taught all aspects of diabetic care, and only needed my evaluation, reassurance and the continuing support of a home health aide. I should explain that Medicare requires a registered nurse to directly supervise home health aides every two weeks. If this is not done, the agency risks not receiving reimbursement. Furthermore, the nurse must document either that the patient is improving or turning worse, with specific measurements, and that a new area of instruction in some related aspect of diabetes has been given. With a sigh of relief at having escaped the apartment building unharmed, I headed back to the VNA office, thinking that this had been a very interesting, but also a very difficult day with many unexpected impacts on my performance.

5. CAUSES OF PERFORMANCE PROBLEMS

The Riverside VNA is in sharp contrast to the Sunshine VNA where I had worked previously in three areas which are critical to an independent contractor's performance. Riverside's patient records were difficult to read through and find the information I needed to conduct a thorough assessment of the patient's main problems. Frequently, I couldn't find up-to-date medical diagnoses, the nursing plan of care for wound care was either missing, non-specific, or inappropriate to the patient's current condition, and I had no idea of other community resources involved in maintaining the patient at home. There were no directions for getting to people's houses. The nurses' notes suggested that they didn't seem to have as good a grasp of all that goes into making successful home visits. Their documentation of care was of the type in vogue many years ago., lacking the precision and thoroughness of today's nursing processes. In reflecting back to that day, I realize I had no orientation to that agency; I simply was assigned the patients, handed the necessary supplies and records and sent on my way.

6. INVOLVING FAMILIES IN PATIENT-CARE NEEDS

October 4, 1991: I again accepted assignment to the Sunshine VNA, although with some misgivings. Despite the fact that I arrived ten minutes before 8 AM, it was after 9 AM before I received my assignment of six patients. The first two patients lived in another small city, some twenty minutes away. The first was a 92 year old lady, bedbound with rheumatoid arthritis, with badly contracted limbs. Mrs. White was developing bedsores. The daughter, Sophie, seemed unable to retain information and unable to really care for her mother; I wondered what had been going on there all those years prior to the VNA's intervention. The house absolutely reeked of urine. Each time I would try to instruct Sophie as to what she should do to make her mother more comfortable and prevent further problems she would attempt to reiterate what I had said, but then would say something rather different, not really apropo. I finally settled on some very simple, basic teaching measures and said that a nurse would return again tomorrow to help her with her mother. Although I had spent an hour in that home, I left feeling somewhat frustrated and wondering if another nurse would be assigned to follow up on my written recommendations.

I had a hard time finding the next patient's house, spending nearly an hour on the road. The tiny, weak, trembling, nearly mute and very sad lady had severe Parkinson's, exacerbated by recent surgery to implant a pacemaker. Miss Gladys lived with her sister and brother-in-law; since her surgery, she had suddenly become totally dependent on them for her care. I did the best I could for Gladys—I assessed her physical status, changed the Tegaderm bandage on her decubitus, and taught measures to promote her return of strength. This was an instance of too early hospital discharge, as well as uncoordinated care on the part of her physicians. Gladys' medications obviously needed adjusting for she was becoming contracted, drooling excessively and having difficulty swallowing. I advised her family to make an appointment with her Parkinson's specialist as soon as possible. I felt that this family was under enormous stress and having great difficulty in coping with their sister's overwhelming needs. They all needed the case management and trust-building skills of a primary nurse. However, this patient did not yet have a primary nurse.

The last patient I saw on Friday had just had a cancerous tumor removed from her perineal area. The huge gaping wound was dressed three times a day with wet to dry sterile saline dressing packings, so that the wound would heal from the inside out. The procedure took at least an hour. By shining a flashlight, I could actually see her bladder way up inside. Mrs.

11

White seemed quite accepting of her home care plan although it was obvious that it would be at least six weeks before that wound closed. Six weeks of having many different nurses come in three times a day for dressing changes of a very personal nature would be quite an ordeal, yet perhaps better than remaining in hospital where she would be exposed to nosocomial infections. Mrs. White knew that after her wound healed, she would have chemotherapy and possibly radiation as well. I asked her son, who readily agreed, to purchase stainless steel bandage scissors for the nurses to use, as the plastic throwaway suture scissors became dull quickly with three times a day sterilizing. Having to utilize dull scissors to cut the Nu-gauze made the dressing change a much longer procedure than necessary. I wondered why no other nurse had made this sensible time-saving request. That was a very tiring day. I didn't leave the VNA office until after 4 PM as there was so much charting to do, my travel time had been extensive, and I had spent much time with each patient, as they were so ill.

7. ENJOYING A SMALL CITY V.N.A.

October 7, 1991: Today I accepted an assignment in a small city VNA, the Walden, and was very pleasantly surprised by the environment there. Although they were renovating their building, with new carpeting being laid, computers being set up, and carpenters, painters, and telephone workmen all milling about in seeming chaos, everyone was most pleasant, calm and well-organized. I noted the presence of an older, very experienced supervisor. The first nurse I saw there was a former student of mine; we enjoyed reminiscing for a few minutes. The patients here are ill, but not nearly as ill as those in the large "Sunshine" VNA. I saw six patients, nearly all of them for dressing changes following surgery. One patient-family in particular, was memorable. She was a young woman of 40 who was bedbound with terminal malignant tumors of the brain; her husband was taking total care of her. While she could not speak, it was obvious that she could hear him speak and was aware that care was being given. She was fed Ensure through a G-tube into her stomach and also medication to prevent seizure activity. I assessed her and found her stable with no impending skin break-downs. The husband was concerned about his medical insurance continuing to reimburse for nursing visits, as there had been no change, either positive or negative, in her condition. However, I was able to reassure him that our visits were absolutely necessary to assess for impending complications and to teach optimal care and that I would document appropriately to ensure reimbursement.

Another lady had had a second radical mastectomy. The second surgery had not gone well; her incision had become infected and she was having drug reactions. I spent about 45 minutes there completing the extensive dressing change, ascertaining her physical status, and being sure that she was taking her meds as ordered. I became aware that this was a tough case with many potential complications and underlying emotional problems, both for the patient and the husband. I could sense his hostility and resentment now that he had to do all the housework, run the errands and cook for them both. The primary nurse would certainly have many factors to consider and address when she returned from her vacation.

The last case for the day was a home health aide supervision visit and dressing change for a middle-aged gentleman who was confined to bed with ALS; he could no longer talk and had a decubitus on his coccyx which was healing nicely with our daily treatments. As his wife worked outside the home, he had a home health aide assigned every morning for four hours. I am impressed with this VNA's ability to provide reliable home health aides for their patients with long-term care needs.

I enjoyed my day at this small VNA; it was really quite relaxed and I was all through seeing patients at 1 PM. I stopped for lunch at a local take-out restaurant and then returned to the agency to do my charting. I'd like to add that this agency's records were the easiest to read and to document in of the three VNA's in which I have worked so far. They have a flow sheet that folds out with listed care plans, such as self-care deficit, ostomy care or mastectomy care plan which makes charting very clear, concise and measurable, allowing the reader to see the progress in the case very easily.

The contrasts among large and small urban and suburban VNA's continue to surprise me. The nurses here at this fairly small agency (Walden VNA) seemed to take enormous pride in their work. Many of them had been employed there for ten or more years. There was a sense of great camaraderie. So far, I would have to say that the smaller the agency, the better organized, and the better the care given. The nurses seem to be accorded more respect and consideration in the smaller agency as well. I wonder what other variables may be in place which significantly influence the quality and continuity of care of patients and nurses' satisfaction with their work.

8. A VARIETY OF VISITS

October 8, 1992. This is my third day this week at the Walden VNA. I am really feeling quite comfortable and relaxed about the nursing care that is expected of me and of the geographical driving lay-out. The first patient I saw this morning was an elderly man with congestive heart failure, who lived with his wife in a one-story spacious ranch. Louis was a retired chef with the usual varicosities of lower legs, old healed ulcer sites and bluish feet and toes. Of Italian ethnicity, his knowledge of English was poor, making communication difficult. His wife was lying in bed; she seemed depressed and couldn't answer my questions appropriately. I had difficulty ascertaining whether or not Louis was taking his cardiac meds; in fact, I think he was having a problem with alcohol. I instructed him several times in the correct medication dosages and tried to emphasize these to his wife as well, but I concluded that this couple really needed a primary nurse and on-going support services if they were to remain in their own home; their offspring also needed to be more involved.

The next visit was to an elderly newly diagnosed diabetic woman whose expressed ignorance regarding her diabetes was surprising. She told me she could have anything at all to eat and that she was feeling fine. I changed the dressing on her leg ulcer and noted that her bare feet were filthy and at risk for infection. I sensed that unless there was a primary nurse willing to spend a great deal of repetitive time with this woman that the necessary lessons to maintain a stable diabetic status would not be learned.

The third lady was a gracious elder living in a rather plush apartment. She had had a total knee replacement several months ago, but had not regained adequate strength in her legs to ensure her safety in bathing herself. Against the advice of her physician, she had decided to take a tub bath. Having difficulty getting back out of the tub, she had scraped her buttocks severely, managing to remove several layers of skin. We were there on a daily basis to dress her wounds and help her to heal without infection.

Another patient, a young woman of 40 years, was suffering from cancer of the lung, inoperable, it having metastasized from the colon. Yvonne also had a colostomy. She was suffering a great deal of pain, for she had fractured a couple of ribs from severe coughing. Yvonne was on Prednisone and morphine to control her pain, but she had severe nausea and had lost 14 pounds in one week. I tried to notify her physician and seek his advice regarding a change from morphine to some other pain-killer, but to no avail. His secretary wanted this very ill and bedbound patient to "go to triage". Of course Yvonne would have had to wait in the emergency room several hours. I did not think that this was a sensible or humane solution. I advised the family to wait for the physician's telephone call, and to offer small amounts of sweet tea or other fluid that this poor woman could tolerate, and to resume her expectorant cough syrup to ease her coughing.

The last patient, a tiny, wizened little Italian woman in her nineties, was being cared for at home by her daughters, who worked in shifts around the clock. This patient was bedbound in the last stages of dementia; she was not fully conscious. The ulcer on her coccyx was healing nicely; however, her daughters said she was severely constipated. Abdominal assessment was negative for any problems, as was a rectal exam. I gave her family some suggestions as to how to better control her bowel movements and complimented them on their superb care of their mother. Then I returned to the office, completed my charting and said goodbye to all of the staff present.

9. EFFECTS OF LONG HOLIDAY WEEKENDS

October 15, 1991. Reporting to the Sunshine VNA, I proceeded to wait one and one-half hours before receiving my assignment. The reason given was that because this was a Tuesday after a long holiday weekend, they were unsure as to which patients needed to be seen. I finally did see six patients, many of whom were quite ill, in three different cities. There were two visits which were particularly notable.

10. EQUIPMENT FAILURE

The first visit was to a newly insulin dependent diabetic; a woman who had had diabetes many years, and whose mother had died of diabetes complications. This woman was in her late fifties; very obese and a severe cardiac. She seemed to have a defeatist attitude about her new insulin-dependent condition. She seemed vague in her comments; almost dazed. I was to begin to teach her how to use a glucometer and the relationship between her blood sugar level and the insulin dosage. She was successful in puncturing her finger to obtain a drop of blood for glucometer testing, but the agency's glucometer I had brought with me would not work properly. This was not the first time that I had encountered malfunctioning glucometers, but it was the first time that obtaining a glucose measurement was so crucially important.

I resolved to purchase my own glucometer as soon as possible, for patients such as the woman above really must be closely monitored while they are adjusting to their new insulin regimes.

I talked with this patient for quite a long time about her diet and other things she could do to promote her health, but I'm not sure she was able to process all of the information. My written recommendation included another nursing visit later in the week to observe for signs and symptoms of hypo or hyperglycemia and to instruct in use of glucometer.

11. SUPERB DOCUMENTATION BY PRIMARY NURSE

Another patient, a delightful gentleman of 78 years, with Waldenstrom's macroglobulinemia, had a very pronounced case of pneumonia. Bert's lungs were just full of crackles and rales from midway down. However, he was responding to the Erythromycin, as was easily determined by comparing my assessment with those of his primary nurse, whose documentation and management of this case were superb. I was successful in gaining for Bert a doctor's appointment in two days' time to determine whether he would then be well enough to undergo plasmaphoresis the following week, as previously scheduled.

12. INEFFICIENT TIME MANAGEMENT

October 17, 1991: I was assigned only five cases at the Sunshine VNA, as two patients had either refused a visit or had gone into the hospital. This meant, that once again, my time was wasted. As I consider my time very valuable, I was experiencing renewed feelings of frustration and annoyance, both of which were extremely familiar to me from past employee experience. I didn't expect these feelings to surface again, now that I was self-employed. Since this VNA had arranged for my assistance two weeks ago, I had expected my assignment to be ready upon my arrival. Furthermore, the first case was an admission which meant three hours of paper work. I rather enjoy doing an admission from the teaching and assessment aspects, but I dislike the amount of redundant paper work at this particular agency.

In their efforts to ensure well-documented quality patient care for the Department of Public Health and insurance reimbursers, this agency has quantities of paper forms to be filled out including nursing diagnosis care plans and flow charts with repeated, repetitive signs and symptoms measurements. The medication pages were the worst—we had first to find the computer code number for each drug listed generically by class, not alphabetically. There were 24 pages with 50 drugs listed on each page. On another page in the patient's record, we then hand-wrote the prescribed brand-name, purpose of the drug, the dosage and schedule, and all of the possible side effects. Some patients had ten or fifteen drugs prescribed. It was obvious to me that whoever designed the drug profile system had no knowledge of the time constraints of community health nurses. I should have been able to see six patients a day and complete all necessary documentation within six to seven hours at most. Instead, I was seeing only five to six patients in eight hours of work.

13. NURSE UNIT LEADERS VERSUS NURSE MANAGERS

This agency, the Sunshine VNA, utilizes unit leaders, rather than nurse managers or supervisors as their daily patient care coordinators and managers of staff. They are young nurses who have practiced for one or two years as staff nurses, and now have been promoted. They have usually had little administrative education for the position. They often visit patients also, which may add to their feelings of overload and role confusion. I inadvertently overheard two unit leaders conversing by telephone with their staff nurses who were resigning. Stating that they felt sympathy for the overwhelming case loads of these nurses, they also emphatically stated that 45 patients on a caseload was the expected norm, and there was nothing they could do about it. Unit leaders' lack of experience and inability to offer wise counsel to their staff nurses often results in high turnover rates among staff nurses. In my experience, frequent primary nurse resignations are a sign of organizational and financial problems as well as a lack of leadership in espousing the rights of individual nurses. I have seen many nurses suffer burn-out from lack of nurturing, caring, and respect for their rights to a reasonable case-load. In addition, a reasonably sized case load is crucial to quality patient-family care.

14. A NEW AND INSPIRING AGENCY

Monday, October 23, 1991. Today I was assigned to another regional urban/ suburban VNA to the north of my home, which I shall call the Lee VNA. What a difference there was between this agency and the Sunshine VNA! Rather than an old victorian house with many flights of stairs to be climbed in the course of obtaining and completing an assignment, along with cramped, inadequate parking space, the Lee agency was housed in a one-story former bank building, with plenty of parking space and ample interior space. There were thirty desks, placed in three rows, with one telephone for every two nurses, three supervisor stations and separate quarters for the administrators and support staff. My impression was of an extremely professional staff, involved and enthusiastic about their work. To my great relief, documentation of patient care has been reduced by about 75% at this agency. They have accomplished this by eliminating the usual required documentation to a single three copy NCR report which documents the patient's condition on that particular day. It describes the patient's physical status, the nursing interventions undertaken, including teaching and the goals planned, and obtains the mutual agreement of the patient and the nurse to the on-going care plan. Then the patient and the nurse both sign this document. One copy remains in the home, one goes into the patient's record and the third copy is the nurse's record of visits made for reimbursement and agency statistical records. Patient participation in the documentation of their care seems to be an empowering experience for both patients and nurses.

15. REFUSING AN ADMISSION

The next week I again accepted assignment to the Sunshine VNA where I had worked previously and was kept very busy traveling to many different towns. I still must wait more than an hour for my daily assignment. I finally refused to do an admission, because the excessive paper work meant that I would have spent two and one-half hours in the office doing repetitive, redundant documentation when I could have been seeing three additional patients.

Refusing to undertake an admission was a new experience for me, as I had always been taught, from my earliest hospital school days, to carry out orders without question, unless to do so would jeopardize the patient's health. My own needs were not usually taken into consideration. Refusals usually meant dismissal or a negative evaluation. I must say that being self-employed seems to give me the power and freedom to stand up for my rights, although my anxiety level zoomed and that old innate fear of disapproval was definitely present in my subconscious mind! In reading Susan Reverby's "Ordered To Care" (1987) I noted that attention to duty was essential: "The Nightingale model thus emphasized character training and strict discipline,—linking duty, obligation and order" (p.43). We were taught to practice altruism and caring, yet were unable to be autonomous beings. No wonder that I, having acquired an advanced nursing education, experienced mixed feelings when working as an independent nurse contractor.

16. NEGOTIATING FOR NEW CHALLENGES

November, 1991: I have now accepted an assignment to contract exclusively with the Lee VNA where I had accepted an assignment several weeks ago. This agency wanted me to work full-time for them on a contractual basis for several months, carrying a case-load. A 'case-load' refers to an assignment of the same patients, who are seen on a daily or weekly basis, and involves trust-building, counseling of patients and families, referrals to other resources, and responsibility for the outcomes of the nursing care plans. However, I did not want to make the investment of being responsible for case management and the attendant documentation. I also feared that the novelty and adventure of seeing a different group of patients each day would be missing. I realized how much I was enjoying being self-employed and able to care for patients in the best possible manner, according to my standards. I also suspected that I would not be compensated adequately for the extra time involved in carrying a permanent case-load. We settled on a three day work week, substituting for absent staff nurses throughout the agency.

17. A VARIETY OF ETHNICITIES

I've now been working at this northern VNA for two weeks, enjoying the variety of cases and socio-economic settings. I am very intrigued with the various ethnic populations: Greeks, Cambodians, Portuguese, French-Canadian, Indian, Vietnamese, Thais, Irish, Hispanic, American Indian, and Scots-English. Every case is different and requires manners and behaviors according to the patients' ethnic customs. Language barriers are common, yet I manage to communicate by gestures, a few commonly known words, and by demonstrating techniques. Occasionally I telephone a patient's relative who speaks English, and who then translates the information to the patient. In multi-generation families, it is often the grandson or daughter who understands English and translates for grandmother or grandfather.

18. EFFECTS OF HOUSING

I often see seven or eight patients a day, when they are residents of large apartment buildings. Sometimes I am in one building most of the day, and then I begin to long for the outdoors. Although seeing many patients in one building is time efficient, there is no time between visits to recover and begin the planning for the next encounter. I do not have a chance to eat my sandwich lunch back in the car until after 2 PM. The patients are usually elderly, many of them living in subsidized converted mill buildings which are quite elegantly renovated. My impression is that these patients feel well cared for and respond positively to our care and teaching. The residents of these converted mills are friendly and helpful to one another, participating in group projects, shopping trips, dining together, and in general watching out for one another. I have to be careful not to inadvertently divulge one patient's condition or changing circumstances to another. This is all in sharp contrast to some other sections of the city, where elders and other chronically ill live in dilapidated single or multi-family dwellings. They complain about their isolation, fear of robbery, and often seem depressed and lonely. Their wounds do not heal quickly and these patients often do not adhere to the plan of care. We nurses spend much time walking to the housing office to obtain and return keys to the residents' locked doors. I again recognized the importance of affordable, attractive, safe housing in promoting and maintaining the health of elders.

19. NUMBER OF CONTRACTOR VISITS- EFFECTS ON QUALITY

I have observed that some contract nurses accept daily assignments of as many as ten to twelve patients, and I have wondered how they have managed to render quality care with visits lasting only 15 minutes. I myself have refused to visit more than eight patients daily as I feel there is considerable assessment, evaluation and teaching to be done, all of which often takes at least 40 minutes. It 's surprising to me, as a former supervisor, that supervisors today routinely assign 9-12 patients to contractor nurses; but I suppose they are under great pressure to be sure that all post-operative patients are seen so that the Medicare dollars continue to flow into the agency and continuity of care is maintained. Perhaps the contract nurses who make more than eight visits a day help to make up the difference in required productivity levels when a staff nurse is absent, attending a conference, or spending the day completing documentation.

20. PATIENTS' MOST COMMON DIAGNOSES

Now that I have been working as an independent contractor for several months, I note that the majority of the care I give is directed toward the teaching and monitoring of diabetics, those with severe cardiac disease, circulatory disorders resulting in leg ulcers and amputations, severe pulmonary disorders, medication management problems, malnutrition, supervision of home health aides and the management and treatment of constipation. Administering enemas in the home presents a variety of challenges, often resulting in an exhausted nurse, but a much relieved patient. The easiest patients for independent nurse contractors (and perhaps the most satisfying) are the post-surgical cases with dressing changes, such as gall-bladder or tumor removal. These patients are often in the younger age groups between 40 and 75, and tend to heal quickly. They often do not have any other complex medical diagnoses requiring medication supervision, instruction to families, resource referrals, and coordination of multiple care-givers. They are often discharged within three to four weeks.

21. EFFECTS OF INCOME ON CARE ELIGIBILITY

The first patient I visited one day lives in a below ground level apartment with her husband. Betty and Bud both have diabetes and are drinkers and smokers. Betty has had multiple sclerosis for many years, and cannot walk alone. The apartment was filthy; empty beer cans and snuffed-out cigarette stubs were everywhere. Betty is not old enough for Medicare; Bud is on social security disability. Their income is just a little too high to qualify for Medicaid. Betty's feet were in deplorable condition; she needed home health aide services badly. My instinctive feeling was that if dependable continuing personal care could be instituted for this woman, that complications would be lessened and perhaps even an improvement in the total family health would result. They both seemed to be lacking in the sense that anyone truly cared about them and therefore (perhaps) felt no responsibility to care for themselves. I bathed Betty's feet for her, taught her about the importance of good skin and foot care and reviewed her meds. I discussed the high cost of two pack a day cigarettes with Betty and Bud and how that money could be better spent on nutritious food. However, they did not seem motivated to make such a big change, so I finished teaching about diabetes, and hurried out of that smoky, filthy apartment, feeling somewhat disheartened about the futility of my visit there and the high cost to the health care system which will be the inevitable result of this couple's neglected health.

22. EFFECTS OF DECREASES IN MEDICAID FUNDING

In early February 1992, it became evident that large cut-backs in the Medicaid case-load would have to be made, as reduced state funding and restrictive guidelines were again adversely impacting the Lee VNA's ability to provide services for the most needy. At this same time, a new supervisor was hired by the VNA; she asked me to assist in determining which patients could be safely discharged, or at least have their visits cut-back without adverse results. I found I was able to discharge a number of patients for many of these persons could be encouraged to attend a neighborhood health center for their care. The plight of the chronically mentally ill patient was different, however. As usual, the amount of money allotted for their care was grossly inadequate, and thus their continuing care needs were often not met, only leading to more complications and frequent hospitalizations.

23. A HARD-TO-BELIEVE EXPERIENCE

March 19, 1992: One visit that stands out today was to a thin, frail-looking man of about 35 who lived with his family in what can only be described as a hovel on one of the oldest streets, really just a narrow lane in the northern part of the city. I was met at the door by a short, stout elderly woman with long, grey-black hair streaming down her back. Greeting me with a blank affect and indistinct language, she led me through the dark living room. When my vision adjusted, I noted two short persons with rather large heads, one man and one woman, I think, who appeared to be mentally retarded and were seated on opposite sides of the room. They did not respond to my greeting, other than to nod their heads. The room was heated by a kerosene fire in a make-believe fireplace. Cigarette smoke permeated the atmosphere and a strong odor of urine assaulted my senses. The woman indicated that I should follow her into the kitchen which was heated with an old black coal cooking stove, the oven door standing open to allow more heat into the room. There were wet newspapers all over the filthy floor, and it was apparent that the cats and dog used these to "do their duty". I was invited to sit down on one of only two chairs at the kitchen table, but given the condition of the floor, chose to place my nursing bag on one chair while the patient sat in the other chair. I stood for the entire visit. Robert's face was badly disfigured as he had had surgery for cancer of the mouth and pharynx. He gestured to me and was able to speak a little. He fed himself with Jette type G-tube feedings. Robert was a chain smoker, despite his ordeal with cancer, but was "trying" to cut down. He was gaining weight but needed further instruction on the importance of cleansing his mouth several times a day with the solution prescribed by his physician. I was very uncomfortable in this deplorable household, and so after complimenting the patient once more on his consistent and carefully done tube feedings, I left this domicile as quickly as possible. And that visit was my astonishing finale for the day.

One doesn't expect to see such a state of squalor and potential for disaster in a large Eastern U.S. city when visiting nurses are involved in a family's care. I wondered if the primary nurse had approached the Board of Health officials concerning the unsafe condition of this family or if the family had refused her assistance in improving their housing situation. One of the difficulties in being an independent contractor is the lack of background knowledge about the overall psychosocial and economic condition of patient- families, for today's patient records do not contain socio-cultural information. Thus I sensed that I probably did not accomplish as much as I could have, if I had been cognizant of the external conditions affecting the family.

24. MULTIPLE MEDICATION MANAGEMENT

Another memorable visit that day was to an elderly obese lady, rather unkempt, dirty and eccentric in her behavior, with severe diabetic and cardiac disease who had imigrated from Russia at age nine years. Helene and her brother James, in his late seventies and none too clean himself, shared a first floor apartment. Their living quarters were totally disorganized and dirty; food spills on the kitchen table hampered my ability to use the surface for writing. Helene had a multitude of medicines, some ten to fifteen different prescriptions, and some over the counter, which were all listed on her med sheet. However, she had been refusing to either take or refill the prescriptions on about half of these. Today Helene complained of continuous pain and burning in her right foot. I explained that if she would take her pentoxifylline (increases blood flow, diminishes intermittent claudication) that the pain might diminish. She then agreed to take this medication and several other important cardiac drugs. She eventually allowed me to order all of these from the pharmacy. Then I proceeded to try to pre-fill her weekly medication cassette, which had dried food blobs in each compartment, as well as some left-over pills she had not taken. As it would have taken me an hour to properly clean the cassette cubicles, I did not attempt this. Helene was prescribed medications four times a day, seven days a week, but only she knew the whereabouts of the pill containers, for she had partially hidden them in various places around the apartment. Eventually, guided by her vague directions, I found all the bottles and filled the cassette, discussing each pill's purpose and necessity in preventing future attacks of angina and other problems. I also filled her insulin syringes for the week and placed those in the filthy refrigerator. I would classify this woman as an unstable angina patient, as she had taken three nitroglycerine tablets for severe chest pain two days ago. She was also a severe diabetic. I could not determine her blood glucose status for she goes to the hospital clinic each month for glucose testing. There were no glucose lab reports in her record. Helene thanked me profusely for my time, concern and teaching, but I doubt that she will follow-through with all of my instructions. Helene's primary nurse will need much tact and diplomacy to achieve some cleanliness in this home, as well as total medication adherence, or else accept the fact that this is the way Helene and James like to live.

25. ON ULCER AND DIABETIC CARE MANAGEMENT

March 24, 1992: Yesterday and today I visited a tiny lady in her 80's who lived alone in a well-furnished second-floor apartment. Virginia has been troubled for the past couple of years with painful leg ulcers. She had had spinal surgery many years ago and her doctors had warned her then that as she grew older she could expect decreasing circulation in her legs with skin break-downs and painful feet. The prophecy was now fulfilled. Virginia's feet had not been bathed in some time, and were not only crusted over with dried debris but also smelled badly as well. I proceeded to bathe her feet in warm water for which she was quite grateful. And then as I set up for the sterile dressing procedure, I discovered to my horror that the gauze pads the nurses had been using were not sterile. These small pads also stuck to the wounds on her legs to the point where it was excruciatingly painful to remove them, even though I doused them with quantities of sterile saline solution first and waited awhile before pulling them away. Fortunately I found the necessary sterile pads in my bag with which to proceed with the Carrington gel protocol. This visit took an entire hour's time.

The following day, Virginia complained of dreadful pain in her legs which she had experienced all night. She begged me to try Telfa pads on her ulcers, rather than the gauze pads which clung to the wounds. I explained the rationale for gauze pads—that they were utilized to debride wounds and provide a healthy tissue base for granulation; but with her continuing pleas, I agreed to try Telfa pads for the following two days to alleviate her pain, allow her to sleep, and to see if more healthy granulation of tissue resulted. I documented this plan carefully for the next contract nurse, so that she would understand and would call the physician if no improvement resulted.

Another tiny elderly lady living in a second floor apartment had just been discharged from a rehabilitation nursing home after treatment for her brittle diabetic condition. Beatrice had stage II ulcers on both heels and stated that nearly all the patients on her floor in the nursing home also had heel ulcers. I found this information rather disturbing, but was truly horrified when I removed her slippers and saw the condition of her feet. They were covered with dry, flaky, scaly skin, were dirty and smelly and had much debris between the toes. Beatrice said her feet had not been bathed, not even washed, for several months. Her many care-givers had each refused, using the presence of heel ulcers as their rationale. I was shocked to think that the physician or the supervising nurse had not insisted on regular foot care while the patient was in the hospital or nursing home.

With the patient's permission, I bathed each foot in warm water, keeping the heels out of the water, dried the feet carefully, removing much debris in the process, and applied a moisturizing cream. She said her feet felt much better—certainly they looked much better, with improved color and texture. I treated the heels with betadine to dry, and then applied duoderm, as ordered. I doubt that this treatment will be effective, as her circulation is so poor, but it's worth a try. I also discussed her nutritional status with her, stressing the need for adequate protein to aid in tissue rebuilding and that she needed to move her legs and feet by means of range of motion exercises many times a day to improve her circulation.

I have noted over the course of the past several months that there is a lack of consistency in nursing documentation and protocols for the care of diabetics. In the front of each patient's record I think there should be listed the range of glucose levels at various times of the day that are acceptable by that patient's physician, and the nursing orders to be executed when the glucose level is out of range for a pre-determined length of time. In addition, the care of leg and foot ulcers need protocols established according to the origin and the stage the ulcers are in so that the nursing care given is completely consistent., and therefore measurable. I also believe that all ulcer care should be undertaken using only sterile supplies, equipment and technique. I have found that some nurses order and use only sterile supplies for the same type of wounds for which other nurses utilize unsterile supplies. I realize that the cost of sterile supplies influences the nurse in some cases, as patient-families will state they simply cannot afford sterile supplies. (This agency does not provide dressing supplies on a long-term basis; patients must order them from their own pharmacies). The nurses also need to be reminded that foot care is an integral part of comprehensive nursing care in the home. Foot care should be written in as part of the nursing care plan when a home health aide is not present, so that both the primary and the contract nurses will perform this essential task on a twice or three times a week basis for all patients with impaired foot and leg circulation.

26. TEACHING CAMBODIAN PATIENTS

The first week in April found me working in various parts of the city, which increased traveling time in my car significantly. The supervisors seemed to be hard-pressed to assign me my desired seven patients a day, for caseloads were down and previously ill staff nurses had recovered and returned to work. However, they not only did not want to lose me to another agency, but I did not want to work anywhere else at present. I felt bonded to this VNA; it was springtime, the driving was easier, and I felt I could handle almost any situation. Thus, I would accept two or three patients from each supervisor. One benefit of many district visits was that I had unique opportunites to care for a variety of Cambodian families.

The first case was that of a tiny Cambodian grandmother, living with her daughter, three small grandchildren and her daughter's boyfriend on the second floor of a tenement building in a three room apartment. This was perhaps the most tragic and grief-provoking of all the families I have visited thus far. Mia could speak no English, but was obviously in considerable pain from the terminal stages of cancer of the liver. Unfortunately she also had hepatitis B; we were concerned that her family had been exposed and possibly could become ill with this highly infectious and dangerous disease. Teaching them how to prevent contracting this disease was difficult, but the primary nurse apparently had had some success in instructing this multi-generation family in preventive hygienic measures. At this time, Hepatitis B vaccine was beginning to be available, but I did not know whether the children had been immunized and I had not yet had my own series of immunization injections. This VNA no longer provided family health data in the patient's record, an omission which indicates how far from community health the VNA has veered—its emphasis now is on acute, episodic care. Grandmother was jaundiced, weak, itchy and suffered much nausea, intermittent fever, and loose stools. She had great pain in her upper right abdomen, radiating into her chest, shoulder and down her right arm. Mia just lay on the sofa, unable to drink enough fluids to prevent dehydration. Although her daughter spoke some English, it was very difficult to make her understand the need to give her mother the anti-nausea medication, and to understand the sequence of the pain meds to prevent further dehydration and subsequent rehospitalization. I finally drew a clock, numbered the medication bottles, and listed the numbers on the clock at the appropriate times. This the daughter seemed to understand.

Another Cambodian, a pleasant young mother with a ten year old daughter, was being treated with an intramuscular injection of a powerful antipsychotic drug each week to control her schizophrenia. She also undergoes renal dialysis three times a week and has a history of tuberculosis. Her clean, but sparsely furnished first floor apartment is shared with her mother, who has a heart condition and I think mental illness, and a brother, who has cerebral palsy. Despite all these family problems, they seemed to be quite healthy and content; the young mother was consistently managing to stay within her restricted diet and fluid guidelines. I had the distinct impression that this family was being well-cared for by their medical and nursing providers.

The third Cambodian, a 55 year old gentleman, lived with his wife and five grown children in a first floor tenement building. This man and his wife speak no English; one of their offspring served as interpretor and administered the insulin to his father each morning, as the father refuses to learn. My impression was that the father expected to be cared for by his son—that their culture demanded this type of dependency when illness occured. Communicating and teaching about the care of diabetes and asthma to a room full of watchful, stoic family members was difficult for me. I was never quite sure whether they fully understood, or whether their financial limitations precluded purchasing sufficient fruits and vegetables. I was also uncomfortable because I could not bring myself to take off my shoes upon entry, which is their custom, for there were cockroaches scuttling across the floor and the apartment was not heated. Building a trusting relationship with people who have differing cultural customs is a great challenge for community health nurses.

27. EFFECTS OF PARALYSIS

On two occasions I have visited one elderly woman, who lives alone with the sole company of her little dog, to supervise home health aides and to change the patient's Foley catheter. This pleasant and stoic lady is totally bed-bound because there are never two care-givers in the home at the same time to transfer her from bed to chair or vice-versa. Eliza is paralyzed from the waist down. Over the years her legs have partially contracted at the knee and become rigid; thus changing her foley catheter has become an ordeal for the nurse. With the home health aide's assistance, we turn this woman on her side, I kneel up onto the bed, using my elbows to hold her leg back toward me, and lift the labia aside in order to view the meatus. It is with a sigh of relief that I finally note pale yellow urine flowing into the catheter drainage tube and am able to climb down off the bed and stretch my aching legs. I wondered how we would prevent the onset of decubitus ulcers, pneumonia, and urinary tract infections in the future in a patient who is so completely immobile.

28. ON CARDIAC REHABILITATION

A memorable visit in an Hispanic neighborhood was to a young man who had had a five way cardiac bypass surgery this past winter and had now developed diabetes as well. He and his wife spoke little English; they have five small children. He is very tense, anxious and frightened about his future. He is still having chest pain; I could not determine why. His blood pressure and heart rate were normal; his facial color excellent. He was taking all medications as prescribed. I doubt that the chest pain was due to angina, but I urged him to report to his physician as soon as possible so that further tests could be conducted. I taught the usual program for cardiac rehab, and he seemed to understand, though communication was very difficult.

29. CAREGIVER DEVOTION

Another visit that day was to a tiny Portuguese elderly woman who had recently suffered a stroke. Emma was also in the last stage of Alzheimer's and totally bed-bound. The hospital bed was set up in the sunny front parlor, which was cluttered with family photos, Victorian style furniture and nursing supplies. She was being cared for principally by a very devoted family friend who was giving her superb care, including G-tube feedings six times daily. Emma is also suffering from a systemic fungal infection. I was there ostensibly to supervise the home health aide, but I didn't arrive until after the aide had left. It is so hard to find one's way around when streets have no sign identification that I am often late for my appointments. I assessed the patient, found her stable and noted that the home health aide's care of the skin was excellent. I reviewed the need for thorough hand-washing and use of gloves with the care-giver friend, and assisted her with transferring the patient to a chair. Most importantly, I complimented her on the excellent care she was giving her long-time friend.

30. CHRONIC MENTAL ILLNESS & INADEQUATE ORDERS

Another visit was to a young 45 year old schizophrenic woman, very obese, who lived in a four story government subsidized apartment building. Doris had recently had surgery to drain a perineal abscess. She was supposed to take Sitz baths three times daily, but could not safely get in or out of her bathtub herself. With only Medicaid managed care coverage, she did not qualify for a home health aide to assist her. Only three nursing visits had been authorized. I was supposed to discharge Doris today, but could not do so, for another cyst had opened in her perineum and was oozing prurulent drainage. I put on gloves and cleaned her up as best I could by asking her to lie down on the edge of her bed and spread her knees apart. I instructed her to change her pad at least three times a day, washing her hands thoroughly before and after. I urged her to return to the surgical clinic for further assessment and to see if she should continue her antibiotic, for I had discovered that she had been taking the antibiotic incorrectly—only once a day rather than the prescribed three times a day. In addition to her antipsychotic medications, I found that she was on a powerful diuretic and had high blood sugar levels from time to time. Doris was trying to lose weight by drinking diet Pepsi and eating doughnuts. Her feet were in deplorable condition, with dry flaky skin and overgrown nails. I wanted to bathe her feet and legs and apply lotion, but this would have taken too much of my time and there was little sense in performing foot care just once. During this period of Medicaid's change-over to managed care organizations, this woman had been admitted to the VNA just for assessment and treatment of her draining wound. There was no mention of her other significiant diagnoses on the referral. Not even her medications, except for the antibiotic, were mentioned on the orders. Thus thoroughly addressing her underlying overwhelming problems was not authorized under the new Medicaid regulations. There was a great deal of teaching and support needed to prevent further complications in this case, but no reimbursement funds nor authority with which to plan a suitable course of nursing care. I felt very frustrated with the limitations of government funding and regulations, for I could predict the onset of diabetes and many more infections from lack of adequate preventive care. The plight of the chronically mentally ill is worsening in this restricted financial climate., where the emphasis is now on instant cure, rather than ongoing care, support and prevention of complications. Upon returning to the office, I discussed this case with the supervisor, who said she would try to obtain additional authorized visits.

31. THE EFFECTS OF DELAYED ASSIGNMENTS

I am now entering my last week of work before stopping for the summer. It is Tuesday, the day after the long Memorial Day holiday, and I am feeling frustrated and annoyed again. Although I arrived at the agency before 8 AM, it is 9:30 AM before I receive a viable assignment, and 10AM when I arrive at my first home visit. I have time today for only six patients, and those visits are rushed—there is insufficient time in each home for optimal care and teaching. Another day during which my standards have been compromised, due to factors beyond my control. However, tomorrow will undoubtedly be a better day, as the Lee agency "gets back into the swing".

32. INSTRUCTING A DIABETIC PATIENT

The next day I was assigned to an entirely new region; thus I spent much time studying maps and finding my way about. It was a good day; however, in that the patients were new and presented interesting challenges. Nine patients had been assigned, but three cancelled. My first visit was to a delightful widow of French-Canadian descent, whose family lived with her in a large scrupulously clean two family house. Evelyn has serious heart disease and insulin dependent diabetes. She asked to be taught how to use her new One-Touch glucometer, developed recently by LifeScan. Evelyn had had this machine for some time, but neither she, her family or other visiting nurses had learned how to use it. Since I have this very same model of glucometer myself, I soon had taught her the basic techniques. I also emphasized the need for at least one of her family to learn the technique and urged that someone be present at the next nursing visit. I felt that the entire family should listen to the audio-cassette which would describe the techniques and rationale for blood glucose testing, for Evelyn had informed me that her deceased husband, and her maternal grandparents had also had diabetes; thus I knew that one or more of her children and grandchildren would probably develop diabetes. Evelyn felt that she had excellent control of her diabetes, for her blood sugar level, three hours after breakfast, was only 87. Knowing this was too low, I suggested that she check her blood glucose level three times, once before breakfast and insulin; another day before lunch and a third day before supper, writing down the results and time of day for her physician, so that he could ascertain if she was receiving the right amount and type of insulin. She said "that's a great idea and the clearest explanation I have ever had about the effects of insulin on my blood sugar level."

I was "in my element" teaching health promotion for the whole family in the tradition of the community health nurse. I went away feeling very satisfied about the hour spent in teaching and counseling this determined and well-disciplined woman.

33. SHORT AND LONG-RANGE GOALS

Recently the Lee VNA developed a new and intriguing method which sets up short and long range goals for each patient. By utilizing these interim and outcome goals each nurse has a clear idea of how soon we can discharge each patient and all that should be accomplished within a specific time period. In addition to goals; however, I think that the admission criteria should include acceptable ranges for blood pressure, heart rate, weight and blood sugar levels so that we know more precisely what we are trying to achieve with each patient. Under the current system, we do not usually know what the physician wants for a fasting blood sugar range, or even a random range. If we knew these ranges in advance, we could proceed with teaching and modifying the dietary plan much more efficiently and with greater assurance of success. The physician's time would also be saved as our phone calls would be decreased. There would be fewer lapses of time during which the patient is "in limbo", and hopefully fewer episodes of hyper or hypoglycemia.

34. ADMIRATION FOR HOME HEALTH AIDES

Another observation is that of the home health aides employed at this agency. They are the finest I have ever worked with—always well-groomed and in uniform. With their neat white plastic aprons donned, they lay out their soap containers, paper towels and gloves upon arrival, and after washing their hands carefully, they begin their personal care tasks in a caring but efficient manner. They stay in the home a full two hours, which enables them to do a top-notch job as well as providing respite for the primary care-giver. I believe the two hour visit also demonstrates that the agency cares about the physical and mental well-being of their aides, who care for just four patients a day, rather than the six to eight patients common in other agencies. The two hour visit also helps the independent contract nurse, who has some flexibility of time in arranging her home health aide supervision visits.

35. THE ENVIRONMENT & EFFECTS ON NURSES

A requirement of community health and contract nurses is that they must provide their own automobiles and pay their own expenses. Driving around in traffic in all kinds of weather, looking for safe places to park, is a hazard and a stress unknown to hospital nurses. In my experience, automobile driving stress is not an acknowledged factor in nursing agencies. Many times I have had to schedule home visits based on the availability of metered parking spaces, or on traffic patterns and one-way streets. I have received several parking tickets, not having placed a sufficient number of quarters in the meter—I underestimated the amount of time needed with the patient. (This agency does not reimburse nurses for either parking violations or use of meters). Other environmental factors which impact the community health nurse include the frequent severe weather changes of winter. Chapped and painful split hands and fingers from all the hand-washing; cold feet and bodies subjected suddenly to the suffocating heat in patients' homes, having to wear winter boots, gloves, hats and heavy coats, all of which must be removed upon entry into the patient's home, and then put on again when leaving, adds to our energy expenditure and shortens the actual visit time.

In summer, our cars become ovens of pent-up heat as vehicles must be locked when parked, usually on treeless streets. Patients' homes are not air-conditioned; thus nurses must have much stamina to cope with the high heat and humidity and physical exertion of climbing in and out of their cars ten times a day, up and down flights of stairs, carrying their heavy bags of supplies and equipment. Lunches are eaten in the car, if at all. Coffee-breaks are unheard of in community health agencies, and lack of bathroom facilities sometimes forces nurses to request use of toilets in patients' homes. All of these environmental conditions necessarily impact the physical health and stamina of the community health nurse and contract nurses, and contribute to the high absentee rate I have observed in this and in other agencies.

36. OBSERVATIONS ON STAFF NURSE ABSENCES

Lengthy staff nurse absences include those due to maternity leave, as well as to acute illnesses. The most common illnesses include bronchitis, pneumonia, thrombophlebitis, gall bladder disease, flu, allergies, facial infections, cellulitis, back strain, broken limbs, car accidents, and family crises. About one-half of the staff at this agency are in the 25 to 35 age bracket, the rest are between 35 and 55. Quite a number are obese, and some are smokers. It appears that this highly professional staff take extraordinarily good care of their patients, but not as good care of themselves. Perhaps the agency itself transmits a conflicting message to the nurse, for revenue needs and required number of daily visits place tremendous pressure on staff nurses to see more patients than perhaps they can physically or emotionally handle.

The risk of serious, even fatal infection to nurses from patients in the community is increasing. I have recently begun my Hepatitis B immunization series, as have many other nurses. Of course, the fear of acquiring the H.I.V. virus by accidental needle-stick or via body fluids is always with us. I am extraordinarily careful with syringes, and always wear gloves now for any procedure which could place me at risk.

37. SUMMARY OF MY FIRST YEAR

Verbally tape-recording and then word-processing my impressions and observations on a weekly basis has been a truly enlightening and rewarding experience for me. This has validated both my work and the concerns I have had as I care for ill patients and deal with difficult situations, including the idiosyncrasies of each nursing agency and its territorial domain.

It has been a very interesting and challenging year. I have had a great many new learning experiences, both in direct patient care and in observing the strengths and problem areas within nursing agencies.

For the majority of this time period, I have felt great satisfaction in being able to practice nursing according to the profession's highest standards of patient care. I have appreciated the autonomy and personal responsibility that independent contracting affords me. However, I have occasionally felt isolated from up to date information about agency protocols and the latest insurance documentation requirements. The most glaring omission has been my lack of knowledge regarding each agency's referral network for outside resources. This has limited my ability to refer patients and families to appropriate providers as needed to prepare them for discharge from VNA services, especially when there is no primary nurse assigned.

It has been gratifying to realize the extent of my professional knowledge and experience. My many years of work in various health care settings has given me the ability to readily discern the nature of a patient-family's lifstyle, to know the appropriate questions to ask to aid in identifying specific problems related to their diagnoses, to modify my teaching style to suit their learning needs, and to be able to enlist and motivate them to restoring or improving their health.

The ability to teach measures toward preventing illness was limited by the exigencies of time, and the lack of documentation significance for insurance reimbursement, for none of the insurors is interested in the prevention of future illness. Prevention of further complications could only be addressed when related to the patient's current acute problem. Thus underlying problems in family nutrition, safety, life-style, or housing which might be factors affecting the patient's own ability to improve his health, could usually not be evaluated nor have planned interventions validated in the documentation. Green and Driggers (1989, p.84) describe the concept of community health nursing as incorporating the community as client and emphasizing the promotion of health. Home health nursing, in contrast, is the care and treatment of episodic illness of an individual patient. It appears that the traditional role and responsibilities of the community health nurse are being lost in the race to provide episodic care to acutely ill individuals.

I made many observations about the nursing agencies' organization, staff abilities, continuity and comprehensiveness of patient care, and nurse satisfaction. Agencies employing mature, experienced supervisors, rather than younger, inexperienced unit-leaders, are at a distinct advantage, for supervisors' wealth of knowledge and training in community health enable them to advise and keep close tabs on their staff nurses, so that grave errors or omissions in patient care do not occur. They are also better able to offer empathic guidance, which all nurses need from time to time. As a contract nurse; however, it was often difficult or impossible for me to verbally report significant patient/family problems to a supervisor, as she often was in conference or on the telephone when I returned from my day's work. Although I left written notes, there was rarely any feedback regarding outcomes of worrisome patient problems.

Over the course of the year, I found that one, large regional agency (Lee VNA) which was computerized and adequately staffed with baccalaureate prepared nurses and three experienced supervisors, offered very good home health nursing care to patient-families and achieved a high degree of nurse satisfaction. I cannot say the "very best" nursing care, for there were many omissions of foot care and not all patients who needed home health aide care had these valuable assistants in place. For most of the time that I was there, the supervisors worked together as a team, sharing each other's nurses when one district was over-loaded with admissions; providing back-up contract nurses when a primary nurse was obviously overwhelmed, and generally maintaining a relaxed, cheerful and cohesive work force. The primary nurses were still making a great effort to provide some health promotion care for their patient families. I observed many instances of well-coordinated case management activities which provided essential base support services for chronically ill, frail and homebound patients.

However, this agency was no longer practicing traditional community health nursing. Well-senior and well-child clinics offering basic health promotion, screening and disease prevention programs were missing. In contrast, the small city agency (Walden VNA) in which I worked not only conducted well-child and well-senior clinics, but also had a cohesive nursing staff. Their camaraderie was a marvel to behold and their patient families were meticulously cared for in the best community health traditions.

Toward the end of my first year at the Lee agency in which I thoroughly enjoyed working, the supervisor with whom I was often assigned accepted another work assignment within the agency. She had been performing the duties of supervisor which also included maternal-childhealth for many years; the director of nursing offered her another position, that of admissions nurse. I was truly impressed, for this nurse was approaching retirement age and showed signs of both fatigue and boredom with her present position. To think that the Director would make such an effort to retain this older woman so that she would be eligible for the agency's pension! My respect and admiration for this particular VNA and its director surged. Thus the older supervisor, whose vast experience resulted in a team of staff and contract nurses who worked well together with daily assignments consistently prepared on time, was replaced with a young master's prepared community health nurse who had not previously been a supervisor. This was when my problems with having patient assignments ready for me and within contiguous areas of the city began to occur more often.

Despite the problems I have mentioned concerning the utilization of independent contract nurses, I believe that independent nurse contracting by experienced community health nurses has become a viable and effective resource for many nursing agencies. There are no overhead benefits to pay, agencies are able to ensure continuity of patient care, and productivity levels are maintained. Primary nurses also benefit from the fresh observations and suggestions of contract nurses in caring for their chronically ill patients. In addition, nurses who are looking for new challenges now have the opportunity to work as independent contractors while they search for permanent employee positions, attend college, or to simply be independent contractors, enjoying the autonomy and freedom from typical employee constraints while benefiting from the variety of agencies, territories and patient-families.

In contrasting large agencies with small agencies, I found that the qualifications and abilities of the staff primary nurses were similar; most held baccalaureate degrees in nursing and were skilled, conscientious and caring. Staff turnover rates were higher in large regional agencies, but their primary nurse case-loads were heavier and their patients "sicker"; bonding and camaraderie were very visible in the small agency. The small agency turn-over rate was low, their patients were not as ill and nurses were more likely to know their patient-families over extended periods of time. Collegial relationships with local physicians were also more apparent in the smaller agency. The large regional (Lee) and the small city (Walden) agencies both employed experienced supervisors; independent contract nurses appreciated the organizational skills of these supervisors very much, and vied for assignments with them.

By the close of my first year of independent contracting I was able to identify several factors within the agencies which interfered with my ability to provide high quality patient care and to feel satisfied with my work. Scheduling of visits in contiguous areas, availability of patient records, driving and home location directions, and lack of knowledge about an agency's resource referral system seemed to be the most influential factors to me at the two agencies in which I preferred to work.

I am; however, looking forward to another year of independent contracting, for the rewards of this type of community health nursing are many. I enjoy the adventure and challenge of new patients, neighborhoods, and territories each day. Next fall, I plan to again work three days a week and to continue to tape-record my observations, to reflect upon them in writing, and then to compare my impressions between the first and second years of independent contract nursing in terms of the dynamic forces influencing agencies, nurse satisfaction, patients' acuity levels, and abilities of contract and primary nurses to provide high quality care. Perhaps I will then be able to make some recommendations regarding utilization of independent contract nurses for the future.

PART II

SEPTEMBER 1992 TO MAY 1993

Julia Stevens, RN, MSN

38. BEGINNING A NEW YEAR

On September 21, 1992 I began another year of independent contracting. This may well be my last year of work as a community health nurse, as I am considering retirement. I am again working with Community Health Network; I agreed to an assignment with Walden VNA where I had been about this same time last year. When I arrived at the agency after a 45 minute commute of 16 miles—the same distance as to Lee, but on narrow and crowded country roads—I found quite a number of changes from the previous year. The vast majority of the staff had turned over. The supervisor had retired, to be replaced by one who left precipitously "due to unfortunate circumstances". The newest supervisor was trying hard to maintain control from her second floor office, which meant she had to climb up and down stairs numerous times a day. The result was chaos in the midst of renovations. I was pleased to see two former students of mine on the nursing staff; however, and they seemed to enjoy their work very much, although they appeared stressed, and stated that morale was quite poor at this time. This was in great contrast to last year. The agency had had to utilize many contract nurses over the summer, which had created a sense of loss of control by the primary nurses, a problem which was exacerbated by an incomplete renovation and an inadequate number of telephones. The nurses still did not have telephones on their desks. I had to search all over the building for an available telephone to arrange appointment times with my patients.

39. A FAMILY WITH MULTIPLE COMPLEX DISEASE PATTERNS

When I finally got out on the road to visit my patients, it felt very good to be working again. I was assigned to nearby towns where I had not been before, so it took me a long time to find some of the homes. One family whom I saw today, a couple in their 60's, in very poor health, lived in a large old Victorian home. They are the parents of seven or more grown children, many of whom take turns assisting with their parents' care. The husband has diabetes with neuropathy in his feet and serious heart disease. The wife, whom I was to see, also has diabetes, but as she ate poorly, needed no insulin at this time. Susan had had a four way bypass, numerous toe amputations, has chronic foot and ankle ulcers, chronic constipation, and was quite ill with severe nausea today. She was lying on a day bed unable to sit up by herself. Theresa was unable to move her bowels independently; a daughter came every other day to administer an enema. I could imagine how difficult this must be for the daughter. The house was cluttered and messy; there was a young two year old grandchild running about. Two of the adult offspring came and went, seemingly without accomplishing anything. I had the feeling that the family was in constant turmoil, trying to help their parents whose needs were neverending. I did my usual assessment, dressed Susan's ulcers, and filled her medication cassette with her numerous capsules and tablets. I attempted some teaching about relief of constipation, but the patient wasn't in the least motivated to make any changes in her situation. I turned to one daughter who was present, but she was preoccupied with her child and phone calls. I suppose that the V.N.A. had attempted to assist the family with services that might prevent further complications, but there was no mention of referral for social service or home health aide in the patient's record. Perhaps this family had exhausted their Medicare benefits and were ineligible for more services. I left that home feeling puzzled and saddened that this couple was going rapidly down hill, and would soon require hospitalization again.

40. EFFECTS OF SOCIAL ISOLATION

Another day I met an elderly couple who lived in a small Cape-style home on a quiet residential street. Mrs. M. was tall, slightly stooped, and terribly thin. Her husband, the patient, appeared dazed, with very sparse language. They seemed socially isolated. I ascertained that their diets were adequate, although I wondered about Mrs. M.'s abilities as an accurate historian. When given the chance, Mr. M. was able to respond appropriately and cogently to questions; but most of the time, Mrs. M. answered for him before he was able to reply. Mrs. M. said that Mr. M. was constipated. He had recently been hospitalized for fecal obstruction. Mrs. M. was terrified that he would again need hospitalization for disempaction. She wanted me to give her husband an enema. He didn't want one, and anyway, I did not come equipped to give an enema and had no doctor's order for one. I did do a rectal exam, which was negative, although she said he had not moved his bowels for five days. I think this couple needs housekeeping and socialization assistance on a daily basis. I sensed a growing anxiety, almost a terror on the wife's part. My nursing notes included a recommendation for the primary nurse to explore the possibility of obtaining a housekeeper, referring to an adult day health center, or some other form of reliable socialization for this isolated couple.

41. VISIBLE EFFECTS OF TRUE COMMUNITY HEALTH NURSING

I visited an Hispanic family one day. Their grandmother, who was visiting them from Guatemala had slipped, fallen and broken her hip. She had had an open reduction, which was healing well, and was newly diagnosed with hypertension. I was glad that I could remember basic greetings in Spanish. The daughter served as interpretor. I was also glad to see that this VNA sees patients who cannot pay. This patient had no Medicare insurance. After assessing her vital signs, general condition and the status of the incision, I drew a blood sample and took it over to the hospital for analysis.

Again, no one objected because of lack of a funding source. I was amazed, for other VNA's where I have worked recently have no free patients. Apparently this hospital and this VNA still receive the benefits of successful United Way fund drives. I was also pleased to realize that although it had been several years since I had drawn blood samples, I had no difficulty whatsoever. Other VNA's have long since given up blood drawing responsibilities, preferring to contract with outside laboratories for this patient service.

This small city VNA tries hard to practice true community health nursing. Despite the agency's difficult past summer, their patient-families are very well cared for in comparison with those of other agencies where I have worked. There seems to be an emphasis on prevention of future problems, and an effort to ensure that the primary nurse feels in control of each case, even down to drawing her own bloods and transporting them promptly to the hospital lab. Nearly every patient whom I saw who would benefit from the assistance of a home health aide or housekeeper, seemed to have one. Meals on Wheels were delivered on time, agency social workers were active, and all patients had had their flu shots. I had observed that well-child and well senior clinics were still being conducted. The community was definitely this agency's client, and their goal was health promotion for individuals, families, groups and the community as a whole.

42. ON NEED FOR "STATE OF THE ART" RECORDS

By September 28th, I am feeling very comfortable working in this small city. The agency seems reenergized now, as the new supervisor takes hold. The staff has recovered from the loss of two full-time primary nurses who left recently. However, this agency is not yet computerized, and their patient record keeping system now seems very old-fashioned and redundant to me, following my year's experience in working at the regional "state of the art" Lee agency. This small one-city agency still requires "S.O.A.P. notes" after each visit, which take a lot of time to write, either in the patient's home or back in the office. The initials stand for Subjective, the patient's comment, question, or complaint; Objective, the nurse's observations; Assessment, the nurse's diagnosis of the problem, and Plan, the nurse's and patient's joint agreement as to the action to be taken. This problem-oriented record-keeping system became popular about twenty years ago, when Dr. Stephen Weed first utilized it in teaching interns the importance of listening carefully to their patients' complaints, learning to judge which of their complaints should have priority assessment and intervention. As a component of the nursing process, the nursing profession now utilizes it extensively in teaching students how to identify the patient's most important problems. For experienced nurses; however, such required lengthy recording seems superfluous to our advanced assessment skills.

Even the agency's flow charts seem superfluous to me, now that I have had so much more experience in home health care. I also have to turn the whole chart around to sign my name, as I am left-handed. I am surprised with myself, for last year at this time I thought this agency's record-keeping system was excellent. I've certainly learned a lot in a year's time about the benefits of computerization and a simplified record-keeping system.

43. STAFF CAMARADERIE

Staff members here are a very chatty group; they want me to report to somebody each day upon my return to the office. Usually; however, there isn't anyone around to whom to report at 3:30 PM. I generally manage to finish up my charts and leave the office before the regular staff and supervisor return in the late afternoon. Verbally reporting the ordinary conditions of patients seems unnecessary to me now; I become impatient with having to stand around and listen to mundane problems; nor do I want anyone to try to recruit me for a staff or on-call position. I find it far more expedient to call in directly to the supervisor when I encounter a patient whose condition is critical or for whom I need an immediate referral. I do leave notes on any patients with changed conditions or other important information on the appropriate primary nurse's desk, and I always replace the "tickle cards" in each nurse's file box under the date for the next visit. We also have to obtain and file all of our own patient charts there; there is often a jam at the filing cabinets when several of us are trying to prepare for our visits or finish up for the day, which takes still more of my unpaid-for time. In contrast, at the Lee agency, one hands the record file clerk a list of patients, and lo and behold, a stack of six to eight records is delivered to my desk in about ten minutes. Clearly, I do not feel "bonded" to the Walden Agency; I much prefer the more sophisticated environment at the Lee Agency.

44. ON QUALIFYING FOR MEDICARE CONTINUATION

One case whom I saw yesterday was noteworthy. The patient was an obese woman in her early sixties, a widow who lived alone in a comfortable first floor apartment of a two family house on a quiet residential street. Sally has C.O.P.D., with oxygen therapy at night and various inhalants, sleep apnea, an ulcer on her right leg, and cardiac disease. Sally stated she has been obese all of her life. Both legs are grossly swollen, with numerous old scars and bluish discoloration about the toes and feet. The ulcer is healing slowly; the nurses now visit only every other day for dressing changes. We are using a new and very effective foam dressing which is applied after washing with normal saline. Sally takes 120mg of diuretic daily, has poor appetite, feels great fatigue and does not eat regular meals. Sally is trying to become eligible for Medicare, as her Champus insurance no longer applies, since her husband's death. The agency's social worker has been helping this woman with the necessary paper-work to qualify for social security disability (she is not yet 65 years old). I was supposed to discharge Sally today, as she has exceeded the number of allowed Medicare visits, but the social worker asked me not to do so, as she needs to counsel and assist the patient for three more weeks in order to complete the complex paper-work. Thus I undertook the task of finding a sufficient number of new problems to qualify our visits under Medicare.

After conversing with the patient a little longer, I decided that Sally's fatigue problem could be due to lack of potassium or other electrolytes, for she takes no potassium supplement, nor does she eat potassium rich foods. Blood tests for electrolytes had not been drawn for many months. After explaining my rationale to her, she agreed to eat a banana and orange daily, and to ask her physician on her next visit if she should have electrolytes drawn. As a contract nurse, I have learned not to try to contact physicians unless it is an emergency situation, for it takes too much of my time, the physician often doesn't trust my judgment, and I might be usurping the primary nurse's responsibilities. Also, requesting the patient to ask her physician gives her the opportunity to address her problem directly with her doctor, thus empowering her.

While we were talking about other additions to her diet, a friend arrived with a dozen doughnuts for which the patient had asked! I was flabbergasted, but calmly explained that these were not the best choices for her. Her reply was, "but I crave them", to which I replied, "persons who eat enough protein do not crave sweets". Sally finally agreed to add a cup of cottage cheese to her meal plan each day. I documented a new three- week teaching plan around her nutritional needs, with goals of decreased doughnuts, daily citrus fruits and protein, with the expectation of decreased fatigue, and a measurement of her potassium level. Together with the fact that her ulcer still had two tiny pin-hole openings, requiring regular nurse assessment and treatment to prevent reinfection, I hoped that this plan would pass Medicare muster and that I had not caused trouble for the primary nurse.

45. ON ADMISSIONS, REVISITED

November 11, 1992. Several weeks have gone by since I last recorded, for I have been away on vacation. Shortly before leaving on vacation, Community Health Network called and said I was wanted in Lee as soon as I returned from my trip. I was delighted with the prospect of returning to this large, regional and well-organized agency. However, my last day of work before going away was at the Sunshine agency, and once again, I did not feel I was treated very equitably. The staff greeted me warmly saying they were so glad to see me again, and then presented me with seven cases, one of which was a full admission. I was appalled, because the admission paper work there is horrendous. I hadn't worked there for nearly a year, and couldn't remember the many finite details their complex record keeping system demands. One patient was way out in Maylin, so it was a long, hard day. In looking back to that day, I do not understand why I accepted the admission case; I suppose I did not want to seem uncooperative, lazy or incompetent. I overheard the supervisor there questioning the team leader about giving me an admission: "Don't you remember that Community Health Network has said not to give admissions to their nurses?" The team leader's response was that she had no choice, for her primary nurses were already taking two and three admissions each that day. I vowed to myself not to accept any more assignments with this agency, for in a year's time, they have made no effort to either stream-line their admission record requirements nor to employ a more adequate number of primary nurses.

Now that I am back in Lee, I am pleased and reenthused, even though there are seven primary nurses out on maternity leave or for other reasons. Three Community Health Network contract nurses are trying to make up for the loss. My first day was hard as I was assigned to a new district with which I was not familiar. After that though, the going became easier as I was assigned to the same district more often. Now I've been there several weeks, and am enjoying myself and the superb organization there. Having three experienced supervisors make a great deal of difference to contract nurses, who operate much more efficiently and give better care when attention to their needs for contiguous driving districts and prior preparation of daily caseloads is met. Most of the primary nurses I met last year are still there, which pleases me, for I believe it means that the administration supports their staff adequately—so unlike many other VNA's.

46. EFFECTS OF PRIMARY NURSE LOSS

One of my most memorable cases occured a week ago Friday. At the end of a long, hard day I had to travel from North Lee all the way to South Lee to re- admit a patient who had been hospitalized for five days. I had great difficulty locating the particular apartment building in which the patient resided, due to lack of visible signs and sufficient directions in the patient's record. Mary lived on the second floor of a somewhat dilapidated complex of buildings, in a four room apartment which was messy and in need of much repair. Mary was obese, and confined to a wheelchair. In addition to her diabetes, Mary had serious heart disease, recurrent urinary tract infections, and a non-healing fracture of her left leg, which was pinned and in a cast for the past year. She had just been discharged once again from the hospital after treatment for a bladder infection and septicemia. She complained of an itchy, vaginal discharge. I wheeled her into her bedroom, assisted her onto her bed, and conducted an exam of her perineam. Sure enough, a quantity of a thick, white cheesy substance was pouring out of her vagina. I cleaned her up, helped her back into her wheelchair and telephoned her physician. He prescribed a vaginal suppository which hopefully would correct her condition. I instructed Mary in the necessary procedure for cleansing and application of the suppository, but she herself would not be able to perform the treatment, due to her obesity and leg cast. We telephoned a daughter who usually visited daily and she assented to care for her mother. I carefully reiterated the dangers of infection to the daughter over the telephone, and reviewed hand-washing, use of gloves and disposal of used materials techniques. Next I telephoned the pharmacy and asked that the prescription be delivered to Mary's apartment. I also noted that the household environment was rather bizarre.

Although Mary's husband was there, appearing very unkempt and dazed, he turned away from me without speaking and laid down on his bed, rather than assisting me with transferring his wife to her bed. A twelve year old granddaughter was flitting about the apartment. A large plastic barrel stood in the kitchen corner, overflowing with smelly garbage and empty liquour bottles. Some of the flooring had been ripped up; the bathroom where I tried to wash my hands was filthy. Cigarette smoke permeated the air. I felt that Mary must have great difficulty surviving, yet it was obvious that she was coping quite well. Mary had good control of her diet, as I discovered in doing a glucometer test of her blood sugar. She had benefited from the assistance of a conscientious home health aide, who had kept Mary's skin in excellent condition. Unfortunately, this aide had been reassigned when Mary entered the hospital five days ago. I telephoned the agency, attempting to have the same aide reassigned back to Mary, but was unsuccessful. Mary became upset, quite understandably. These short hospital stays certainly do undermine nursing care plans and personnel, totally disrupting continuity of care. I wondered if perhaps Mary was one of the patients without a primary nurse to keep tabs on her, for a competent primary nurse would have spotted the beginning onset of cystitis, collecting a urine sample and notifying the physician. Hospitalization could well have been averted. I was in this home more than one hour, and felt totally exhausted by the time I left. It was growing dark outside, and I still had to negotiate the heavy commuting traffic back into the city, complete my charting at the agency, and drive home.

47. COMPREHENSIVE CARE FOR COUPLES

Another common occurence throughout the Lee area is that of both husband and wife being confined to bed and chair, living alone, with a succession of homemakers and home health aides caring for them. One memorable day, I went to visit a patient with multiple ailments, including inability to walk alone, in order to supervise the home health aide. The family's home was on the outskirts of the city, attractive, clean, and on one floor. The patient's severe arthritis necessitated daily home health aide care. I then looked across the room and to my astonishment, there was her husband lying in a hospital bed, also looking clean and well-cared for, but unable to even turn over by himself. Another home health aide was assigned to his care. I learned that several nieces and nephews assisted in coordinating this couple's extensive and complex care. The VNA is to be commended for being able to consistently provide continuity of care for this couple and many others in similar situations.

48. IMPACT OF EXTENSIVE MEDICAL CONDITIONS

Another day, I was assigned an admission case. The tall, obese, articulate, single man lived alone in a cluttered, unkempt basement subsidized apartment. Sam had just been released from the hospital following another episode of pneumonia, advanced COPD, hypertension, angina, post CABG surgery, and diabetes controlled with oral medication and a rigid diet. Sam informed me that his extensive medical history began at birth, when he weighed just one pound- sixty years ago. I was astounded, for I didn't think any premie weighing just one pound could survive, particularly sixty years ago when there were no real therapies or oxygen treatment available. He now weighed 263 pounds, and could barely walk. Sam had had a stroke six years ago, with resulting left leg disability. He needed a brace and crutches in order to move about. He sits down beside his stove in order to cook his meals. He has both Medicare and Medicaid; he is considered totally disabled. I could tell from the way he looked and talked that he had an extensive alcoholic history. Sam volunteered that he hadn't had a drink for 11 years. Sam also was a smoker, but had cut down from 4 packs a day to 3-4 cigarettes per day. It's incredible to me that this man has survived so long. Sam was a charming man who said he was devoting his life now to helping others—those with severe alcoholic or smoking problems. He belongs to two support groups; one is called Renaissance where he volunteers as a counselor.

My interview with Sam took two hours' time, due to his extensive medical problems and lengthy list of medications. Toward the end of the interview he became very fidgety and couldn't talk with me anymore; he removed himself to watch television in the other room while I listed his meds on two full sheets of paper. I noted that he was on double doses of most of his cardiac drugs because of his huge size. I next referred him for resumption of his homemaker services in order to have his apartment cleaned and groceries purchased. These phone calls took another 20-30 minutes of my time, as I was placed on "hold" for about 10 minutes, disconnected, waited for a line to be available, and finally was able to refer him to his case manager at Elder Services.

Back I went to the office, where I found to my dismay that the office had closed, due to the staff Christmas party; I was unable to complete the admission process that day as the car was too cold and cramped for me to sit there and write legibly. As I did not work the next day, it was two days later before I was able to complete this admission. On Friday, I also had another new admission to complete. This is the sort of frustrating and infuriating situation I have often found myself in; and I suppose other independent contractors have also. It can be nearly impossible to be efficient and complete admissions in a timely and cost-effective manner. Subconsciously, I always feel as though I have been derelict in my professional duty in not handing over the completed record promptly. This attitude of course, hails back to my student nurse training days, where one never left the hospital ward until one's charts were completed for the day. I have also begun to suspect that the most time-consuming admissions are now given to contract nurses, in order to relieve primary nurses. However, contract nurses are paid by the visit only—an admission visit is $35.00— certainly not compensating adequately for the 3-4 hours spent on the interview, driving time and documentation.

49. ON CONTRACTOR AS CASELOAD MANAGER

I have now agreed to accept a caseload of patients in the Hebron section as the agency is again without a primary nurse for that district. There are a great many chronic, long-term care patients there needing home health aide supervisions and new ideas for maintaining these patients safely at home under Medicare reimbursement restrictions. It would mean more time spent in careful physical assessments, and possibly rewriting nursing care plans to re-qualify the patient under Medicare. After I returned home though, I realized that I would have to discuss with the supervisor how I would be reimbursed for the extra case management time I would spend in caring for these difficult patients. I will discuss with her the possibility of charging the agency for one hour's extra time per day for case management, and see how she responds. I know from experience that this agency is very reluctant to reimburse for any extra time spent beyond the per visit rate. As it turned out, the supervisor with whom I was assigned was absent on my next work day—I never did have a chance to discuss payment for extra hours of case management time before I was reassigned to another district.

50. A GOOD SWIG OF COUGH SYRUP

On Friday I visited for the third time a 90 year old lady who is confined to chair and a few steps with a walker to her wheelchair. Sarah lives alone on the first floor of a two family house, has never married, and has no relatives to watch over her. She is terribly crippled with arthritis, has a severe humped-back, and a fractured pelvis which has never healed correctly. She has considerable pain but takes only an occasional acetaminophen. She has chronic congestive heart failure, is incontinent and has frequent urinary tract infections; she wears a protective pad at all times and is very prone to skin breakdowns, as she sleeps sitting up in her chair. Sarah has a home health aide who cares for her every morning. Three days a week a homemaker arrives at noon to give her lunch and do the shopping and cleaning. Another home health aide arrives at 6 PM to give Sarah supper and prepare her for sleeping. Sarah is very hard of hearing, cantankerous, and tends to be resistant to suggestions for improved nutrition, or to take an antibiotic for the prescribed length of time. She refuses to consider a hospital bed, which would be so beneficial for her.

Today Sarah's lungs have considerable rales in the bases, her ankles are slightly swollen, and she has a congested-sounding cough. I again urged her to take her antibiotic three times a day, carefully explaining its purpose, but she said the pill was too large to swallow. (Indeed, the tablet was huge and uncrushable.) There was a bottle of liquid antibiotic in the refrigerator; this she also refused to take, disliking its taste. She then showed me her bottle of an expectorant cough syrup. Sarah was able to twist open the cover, but could not measure out with a teaspoon, as her hands are too crippled with arthritis. I suggested that she take a good swallow of the syrup every four hours to facilitate coughing up the phlegm, and she said she would do so. I informed her I would return next week, and if she was no better, I would have to call the physician for his advice. I knew from experience that her physician would be most reluctant to either make a home visit or to hospitalize her, as her condition was not yet serious enough and there was no new diagnosis.

51. CHRISTMAS EVE VISITS

As it turned out, I was unable to visit Sarah the next week, as I developed a severe cold and missed work on Tuesday and Wednesday. By Thursday, which was Christmas Eve, I was much better, or so I thought, and offered to work, as the agency was desperate for assistance, and I was feeling guilty for having had to cancel two days' assignments. Again, that old "duty" response taking hold! Unfortunately, I was not assigned to Hebron, but to another district with which I was not very familiar. It took me a long time to see the seven patients whose homes were spread out over many miles. I then dashed back to the office only to discover that it had closed—of course it was Christmas Eve, but no one had thought to tell me that I should just go home and bring the records in on Monday. It was really infuriating, as my last visit was way over in Westy, quite close to my own town, and I had driven all the way back to Lee.

One of my observations about the patients that Christmas Eve was that they were very eager to see me and talk—there's something about holidays that makes patients feel more lonely and forgotten; most of them lived alone and were quite isolated. I admitted one patient to service, a 93 year old thin elder who could barely walk and was quite deaf. Her primary diagnosis was ataxic senile gait disorder. She apparently had fallen to the floor in her apartment and lain there for two to three days before being found by her homemaker.

Her daughter, in her 70's, who did not look very well, had just flown in from California to help her mother for a few weeks. Elizabeth's admitting diagnosis at the hospital was toxic encephalopathy. She probably had taken too much of her cardiac medication and may have had a T.I.A. as well. Elizabeth has a good appetite, but I am not sure she can remember her medications. At present she is prescribed just one Ecotrin daily, and a Nitro-patch to be applied each morning and removed at bedtime. She probably will do well while her daughter is there, for she will have much needed support and socialization. Unfortunately, the patient refused a home health aide, who could have provided her with the necessary long-term support, physical care, medication reminders and socialization she so obviously needed.

52. COMMON COMPLICATIONS OF DIABETES

I also saw an elderly diabetic male patient that day who had recently had an amputation of his lower leg, which had been necessary because of gangrene, which had set in following a prostatectomy. The amputation site became infected; we were performing twice a day sterile cleansing and dressing changes. I found; however, that the dressing had fallen off during the night, and the incision site looked clean and practically healed—no sign of lingering infection. The wife said the doctor had phoned and changed the orders to phisohex cleansing and dry sterile dressing. The wife had purchased all supplies except sterile gloves, saying they were too expensive. We agreed that clean technique would be sufficient at this stage of healing providing the wife thoroughly washed her hands before laying out the supplies and donning non-sterile gloves. I demonstrated all of this procedure and she seemed perfectly capable of following through. I then wrote the orders for the physician to sign later.

Another visit that day was to an elderly lady in a subsidized housing project way out of the city. I found I had to park in a designated space a very long walk from the complex's main door. The weather had changed abruptly and it was now freezing cold with a stiff wind blowing and occasional snow flurries. I still had a bad cold and began to be very sorry that I had volunteered to work on this frigid Christmas Eve. The patient was a long-standing diabetic with dreadfully swollen legs and painful open ulcer areas. I dressed her ulcers for her, measured the diameter of her ankles, and decided to weigh her, as this had not been done in some time. We discovered to her delight that she had lost several pounds on her new powerful diuretic regime. I was able to assure her that the diuretic was working well, if slowly, and to keep up her good dietary and medication regime. I left feeling satisfied with the value of this visit.

I then drove out to Westy, to another housing for the elderly complex, and again had difficulty finding the correct entrance. I had to drive all the way around the complex, park well away from the doorway, and then walk about a hundred yards and then climb upstairs to her apartment. This lady was a 71 year old juvenile diabetic who stated that everything had been going wrong lately for her. Anna's brittle diabetes caused her blood sugars to fluctuate widely; she had had a sudden total loss of vision in one eye last week. She had seen her opthamologist who told her that the vision would return, but when she inadvertently read his notes, she found that he had written that her vision was deteriorating. This apparent deception upset Anna greatly and she was understandably anxious about the true status of her vision. I couldn't help her with her eyesight, but I was able to congratulate her on her eight pound weight loss this week; she adhered strictly to a 1500 calorie diabetic diet, even though she still baked sweet breads for friends. Anna asked me to have a cup of tea with her, and I decided to break my rule of never socializing with food or drink with patients. It was, after all, Christmas Eve. She was very lonely, anxious and needed to ventilate to someone. She was a lovely person, and we had a nice chat. I didn't think it appropriate to address Anna's fear of going blind, as that would have taken much time and I could not follow through. I noted this problem for the primary nurse, and moved on to still another elderly person living alone in the bleakest, lowest income subsidized housing complex back in Lee.

There are always a number of unkempt, rather forlorn men of varying ages standing around in the front hall smoking in this huge, ugly building. I am slightly apprehensive as I walk by them, but have never been approached. I had to take an elevator to the third floor, walk the entire length of the corridor, and then take another elevator to the seventh floor. I felt very alone and longed to go home to safety.

Lucia turned out to be a pleasant woman of Greek origin, in her eighties, who had recently lost her brother and sister. Diabetes was no longer her chief problem, for she had just been diagnosed with cancer of the ovaries, inoperable. She was receiving chemotherapy. A part of that protocol was a daily injection of a serum for ten days. This new drug stimulates the bone marrow to produce more neutrophils, which boosts the patient's immune status. It would seem so cost ineffective to go in every day just to give a sub-cutaneous injection, but of course we do a number of other things while we are there to check on the patient's total well-being. These include vital signs, appetite, bowels, fluids, signs and symptoms of untoward reaction to the chemotherapy or infection. Apparently Medicare has been persuaded to reimburse for sub-cutaneous injections when nurses can document other skilled procedures in addition which will enable the patient to progress. Then I traversed the two elevators again, got back into the car and headed for the V.N.A.

53. ON SAFE-KEEPING OF PATIENT RECORDS

As I have mentioned before, the agency was closed again. They had forgotten to tell me that on Christmas Eve they closed early. I hadn't finished my charting and didn't even have a day sheet with me, and as it was too cold to sit in the car to chart, I took all charts home with me, where they sat until the following Tuesday, four days later. I always feel so uneasy having patient records in my home, yet I really had no choice. To protect patients' confidentiality, the Department of Public Health frowns on nurses taking records into patients' homes, and prohibits taking records to the nurse's home.

54. A HORRENDOUS SITUATION

After Christmas, I again accepted an assignment in the Hebron district, a once genteel neighborhood, now reduced to lower socio-economic class on many streets. One patient, whom I had seen and described in this journal last year, occupied several hours of my time one day. Eliza was in her 70's and lived alone in a small cape-style home on a quiet residential street. She had been bed-bound for several years now, due to paralysis of her lower extremities, and had no bowel or bladder control. Over the course of the summer, Eliza had developed two large and very deep decubitus ulcers on both heels. The left leg was extended completely with the foot pronated and the ulcer on this heel was stage three-four, not infected, with a moderate amount of sero-sanguinous drainage, and a firm eschar in place. We were using daily wet to dry sterile saline dressings, preceeded by a hydrogen peroxide cleansing. This ulcer was healing nicely, if slowly. The other ulcer on the right heel; however, was extremely necrotic. Over the course of the summer, the right leg had become flexed at the knee, so that the heel was constantly on the mattress, nearly tucked under her buttock. Then, too, both legs are so rigid, that they touch one another and are nearly impossible to separate for bathing, peri care and catheter changes. The right heel ulcer was stage five; I could see the heel bone, muscle and fascia. The sero-sanguinous drainage soaked right through a thick dressing and towels and soaked the bed linens. The odor is dreadful; it is obviously infected. The redness, heat and swelling extended right up beyond the ankle bone. She complained of nausea and was unable to eat. There was not much urine in her catheter bag. She looked very ill and was running a fever. I could not change her dressings, as there were no supplies left. Eliza said they had been ordered yesterday, but had not yet arrived. I called the pharmacy and was informed that the supplies were on the way. I decided to return at 2 PM to complete the dressing changes, and asked Eliza to drink as much fluid as possible. She also told me that several days ago, a nurse had attempted to change her catheter, and had "hurt" her in the process, finally calling upon the physician for assistance. The physician is a man of great compassion, evidently, as he came and inserted the catheter, as he has done on other occasions. I assumed that the physician had also assessed her ulcers and general condition. I decided that Eliza probably had a bladder infection now, due to the multiple attempts to insert her catheter.

When I returned at 2 PM, Eliza told me she hadn't been able to drink more than a few sips of gingerale; I noted that the urine was dark orange and she had produced only a hundred centimeters. Worst of all, the dressing supplies hadn't arrived. I was truly in a bind. The physician orders were for only one visit per day, and here I was, making two visits, and unable to perform the procedures which were the purpose of my visits. The patient had active bowel sounds, and there was no abdominal tenderness on my palpation, yet I knew she was very ill from her facial appearance—she looked extremely ill. When I looked at her right heel area, I decided to call the doctor immediately, for the stench and the redness were much worse. I was concerned that Eliza might have septicemia and would need antibiotics very quickly to save her life.

I contacted her surgeon who said she should be admitted to the hospital right away for I.V. antibiotic therapy, but that I was to contact her attending physician who would undertake the actual admission process. It took a long while to reach the physicians, explain the situation and obtain concurrence. Then Eliza's physician had to talk her into agreeing to hospitalization via the telephone. I then called the ambulance, and while waiting for it, made numerous other phone calls. I called the supervisor at the V.N.A. advising her of the events, the homemaking agency to cancel the evening homemaker's visit, to Eliza's family to inform them of the impending hospitalization, then to the VNA to cancel tomorrow's home health aide. I cancelled the delivery of the dressing supplies, since Eliza wouldn't need them after all, and managed to change the left heel dressing with supplies from my bag. I improvised a dressing for the right heel, opening up gauze sponges, and using lots of tape, as there was no Kling for wrapping. I just couldn't send her to the hospital with such grossly soiled dressings. I surmised that this dressing would remain intact for about an hour—long enough to get her into the hospital, and that the nurses there would realize that I had done my best to care for Eliza. I assisted Eliza with collecting items for her pocketbook, straightened up the room, and answered the phone several times. I was there about an hour and a half before I saw her safely into the ambulance. Then I made up the bed, turned off the lights and locked the door as I left.

This whole episode left me with very mixed feelings, including those of anger, regret, relief, and pride. Regret for having to send her into the hospital, yet relief in knowing that's where she needed to be. Anger too, for having to spend so much time acting in the capacity of a primary nurse, and recognizing that the nurse who had cared for Eliza the day before had ducked her responsibilities, including those of having adequate dressing supplies on hand. I also knew there was little chance that my compassion and sense of duty would be acknowledged by the agency or reimbursed adequately. When I returned to the agency, I wrote an order for the extra visit for the doctor to sign, documented two visits on my day sheet and added an hour of case management time, which I felt completely justified in doing. The supervisors were most appreciative of my decision and follow-through in getting the patient to the hospital, but were not willing to authorize the extra case management time, saying that Community Health Network would have to be responsible for the extra pay. I began to feel very upset. I could have just walked away from that patient situation, for it wasn't really my responsibility as a contract nurse to make all those phone calls, nor to make the second visit. But in my capacity as a professional nurse, how could I not care for her to the best of my ability? Now if Eliza had just been left there, she probably would have died during the night, and the VNA could have been sued for negligence. The VNA's reputation with the hospital and the physicians would also have been severely damaged, so I would have thought the VNA would be doubly grateful, instead of treating me as though I had given unnecessary care in order to earn more money.

55. CAN NURSES COMPLAIN WITHOUT
RETRIBUTION?

When I returned to my home, I called Community Health Network (C.H.N.), and they said I had done the right thing, and would be reimbursed. I also asked them if I was supposed to be completing the "486's", which are every sixty day physician order renewals, and which I considered extra paper work for which I was not reimbursed. C.H.N. said this was not part of their contract with the VNA, and I should either not be doing them, or be reimbursed. I felt relieved that I had at last had the courage to lay all my complaints on the table, but I felt uneasy about my future at the Lee agency. As we shall see later on in this journal, there was an apparent repercussion, but I will never know whether it was directly related to my complaint.

56. WORKING ON NEW YEAR'S EVE, TOO!

I volunteered to work on New Year's Eve as one of the supervisors said she was desperate for help. This was not a wise decision on my part, for it meant that I would be working three days in a row. I said I could see only six patients, as I needed to be at home with my family. The patients all lived in Downey, and were not familiar to me, so that meant extra time spent in locating their homes and identifying their problems. I realized mid-morning that three work days in a row were too much for me—I was tired. It was very cold and raw outside; the driving on icy, snowy roads was difficult. Again, I think my senses of duty and responsibility are overblown, but the result of my early training years. Is altruism too high on my list of nursing values? I don't really think so, for at least I almost never leave work with guilty feelings.

57. CARING FOR AN A.I.D.'s PATIENT

One of the patients was a full-blown AIDs patient with dementia. Although I had not cared for any young women previously with AIDs dementia, I had done a great deal of reading, and thought I understood the medical and psycho-social conditions involved, as well as the importance of preventing further complications. This young woman had had a great many complications already; she was on several medications to prevent further problems. I didn't understand the purpose of all the drugs, but she seemed to adhere to her regime. I also wasn't able to do much teaching with her, due to her limited ability to remember and comprehend. I did compliment her on the cleanliness of her home, her ability to take her meds correctly, her efforts to eat adequately, and the obviously loving care she gave her young child.

58. CONCENTRATING FOR MEASURABLE RESULTS

The other five patients I saw on New Year's Eve were also very ill with complex diagnoses, plans of care and anxious families. Each situation took much thought, energy and concentration as I worked to achieve some measurable result and to reassure and teach the families. I was relieved when that day was over, and pleased with my work. In reading Stuart-Siddall's book, "Home Health Care Nursing" (1986), I note that she describes the qualities of a competent home health care nurse as including those of "sensitivity, flexibility, adaptability, and a large dose of common sense. Empathy…working one to one and understanding the client's problem and point of view are elements of concern. It can be wearing on the nurse, and she has to give a great deal of herself in this role." (p. 157)

Julia Stevens, RN, MSN

59. EFFECTS OF HOUSEHOLD SMOKING ON THE NURSE

Now it is Wednesday, January 6th. I am becoming aware of a new problem for me that is occuring as I visit families who smoke cigarettes. Even though I am now asking them not to smoke while I am there, I find that I begin to cough and not feel well soon after leaving their homes. I also develop some discomfort in the sternal area of my chest. I wonder what will happen to me if I continue to inhale all this secondary smoke. It's difficult to request that patients not smoke in their own homes—after all, I am the guest, and am only there with their acquiescence. I think that agencies should make no smoking a condition of acceptance for nursing services.

60. INFECTION CONTROL

Another critical component of home health care which I want to describe is the extreme precautions that we, as home health nurses take to prevent infection from spreading to the nurse, family and to the community at large. Universal precautions, or infection control involves a great deal of teaching and uniform adherence on the part of nurse, patient and family. In doing wound dressing care, we always wash our hands before touching the patient. We then don unsterile gloves to remove the soiled dressing, which is then placed in a non-permeable plastic bag. The contents of the bag are then doused with a bleach solution 1:10, which must be made up fresh each day. Then this bag of soiled dressings is placed inside another bag, tied securely and placed in a sturdy trash barrel for incineration.

The wound care is carried out in various ways according to the physician's orders. Sometimes a cleansing solution is applied first, or perhaps an ointment, or a wet to dry sterile saline dressing is ordered. All of these dressing procedures are carried out using sterile gloves and technique. Often a disposable plastic apron and even a face mask are donned for protection from splashes and air-borne contamination. When finished, we wash our hands thoroughly again. Disposal of syringes and needles is another part of infection control. We bring our hazard containers into the home with us and dispose of the syringe instantly by dropping it into the container without trying to recap the needle. This helps to prevent accidental needle pricks. For patients who are on daily insulin, we ask that they place their syringes in a plastic container and cap it tightly when full, then place it in the trash for incineration. In conducting glucometer blood-sugar tests which I do many times a day, I always wear gloves, place my equipment, including the hazard container, on a paper towel, and dispose of the lancet in the hazard container. The used alcohol sponge, cotton ball, and glucose stick are all rolled into the paper towel and along with the gloves are placed in a plastic bag, tied securely, and placed in a sturdy trash container.

61. ON UNSANITARY CONDITIONS

I should add that unsanitary conditions are prevalent in many patients' homes; there may be no hot water for hand-washing, or the patient may not have all the necessary supplies on hand. Bathrooms are frequently filthy. We bring our own liquid soap and paper towels. The patient may also be sitting or lying on a very low bed with no table or chair nearby on which to set up the sterile field for dressing changes. Frequently the lighting is inadequate; I often ask a family member to hold my flashlight while I proceed with wound packing or catheter changes. We are constantly improvising and making do with less than satisfactory conditions. There have been some homes in which I did not dare to sit down for fear of becoming infested with lice or having my clothing soiled. This is all part of the challenge of home health care and I am usually intrigued with the variety and the ingenuity required of this type of nursing.

62. EFFECTS OF WINTER WEATHER

The month of January 1993 has been very cold and I feel my energies ebbing at the close of every day. I wonder if I even have the energy to make that last visit. Yesterday was particularly difficult. I had eight patients assigned, and I managed to see all of them, but I am paying the price today. I feel emotionally and physically exhausted; I cannot summon the resources to describe the many challenging experiences of yesterday, and so that day will unfortunately be lost forever to the annals of nursing history.

63. REPERCUSSIONS & QUALITY OF CARE

An event happened a week ago at the VNA which I want to describe. I am uncertain as to the reasons for its occurence, but I have two possible explanations. I was asked by my favorite supervisor to take over a caseload in the Hebron section of the city, as they were short two primary nurses and needed a contract nurse on whom they could rely for consistent three day a week attendance for a month's time. I knew that she valued my work with patient-families; a mutually trusting relationship had developed between us—or so I thought. Although I do not enjoy case management any more, I agreed to a caseload of mostly chronically ill, complex patient-families, interspersed with a few post-surgical cases, out of a sense of allegiance to this particular supervisor. I managed that caseload for two weeks, expending extra time and energy on redesigning care plans to meet new Medicare requirements. I experienced a constant battle with myself as to how much actual case management time I should engage in, for I realized that this activity was no longer a priority with the VNA, nor would I be compensated for the extra time spent. As the patients were all in one contiguous area, I was able to visit eight patients a day, including two or three admissions each week. I was trying very hard to duplicate the work of the other contract nurses I had observed in action, without compromising my professional values to any great extent. It is not very enjoyable to work with such conflicts in value, yet if this was the real world of nursing today, I would put up with it for awhile to see if I could keep the same pace as the younger contract nurses.

On the third week I arrived at the office on Tuesday expecting to see the eight patients whom I had told I would see that day, only to discover that two other contract nurses from C.H.N. had been assigned to my Hebron caseload. This meant that there was no opportunity for me to say goodbye to my patients; I wondered how they felt when still another new nurse telephoned; surely these patients must begin to feel "used and abused" by such an impersonal system of care. I was reassigned to Billings, the town I least liked because of its poor street layout, lack of signs and long distance driving. My desk was changed to a place at the rear of the room, for I was now in the domain of another supervisor. I did not know the staff there which included physical therapists and newly hired primary nurses. This event both surprised and dismayed me. I felt devalued—was I as a person so unimportant that no explanation or thanks was needed or was I being subtly punished for previously speaking up about the "486" extra paper work? I tried to quell my feelings of resentment and anger by thinking of a logical explanation for management's decision to abruptly reassign me.

Probably the administration's efforts were being directed toward attaining ever higher productivity levels in order to increase insurance reimbursement revenues and thus cover high overhead operating costs. Certainly the atmosphere there and behavior of the management team had become more and more concentrated and strained over the past few weeks. I rarely heard laughter now; the sense of collegiality and of mutual mission to provide top quality care were now missing. The other two contract nurses are willing to work every day, visiting eight to ten patients, and to do the extra paper work with no complaints. Perhaps this VNA has now been coerced by outside market forces to compromise its reputation for comprehensive nursing care by utilizing contract nurses as make-shift primary nurses. If so, I would expect that the reputation of the VNA for giving high quality and continuity of care will surely suffer in the community and among the physicians. I later heard many patient-families complain about the short and impersonal visits of these contract nurses. These contract nurses are not expected to build trusting relationships with their patient case-loads; most perform minimally in respect to referral to other community resources or to identifying and teaching preventative health measures that patient-families may need, even though they have ostensibly accepted case management responsibilities. In their defense; however, these temporary "primary nurses" are not compensated at a rate that would be commensurate with a staff primary nurse's salary and benefits. Thus contract nurses who assume primary nurse caseloads probably do not feel accountable for extensive case management.

I will never know the exact reason for my being reassigned, for there was not time that particular day to arrange an appointment with the management team and ask for an explanation. By the time I returned to work the following week, the events of the past week were history—the pace of work is so rapid and hectic, and the number of staff and contractor changes at this VNA so frequent, that no one would remember specific details, nor would they think my concerns very important.

The last three weeks I have been assigned to various towns around Lee and have seen a variety of patients, although the number of patients seen each day has fallen to five or six, hardly making it worthwhile for me. On the other hand, I can spend more time with each patient, and have additional time in the car to reflect on each case and to plan possible interventions for the next cases. It is less stressful work in some respects, but the chief benefit to me is the opportunity to perform optimally with each patient-family. All of this time, the two contract nurses assigned to Hebron are seeing eight to ten patients a day. I presume that the supervisors are under great pressure to be sure all patients are seen, and as long as the correct documentation appears in each patient's record, no matter how brief or superficial, Medicare will continue to pay. It's just too bad that the patients do not get thorough assessments and don't have a nurse there who is willing to sit and discuss their problems and help them arrive at solutions. It has become apparent to me that the role of an independent contractor is expected to be limited just to the technical tasks ordered. I should refrain from thinking in terms of community health nursing. I suppose I am experiencing "role confusion". It is very difficult for me to deny my knowledge and practice experience of community health nursing standards just because I happen to be an independent contractor.

I suppose that this diminution of professional comprehensive nursing care will continue and even escalate as long as Medicare continues to pay only for acute care rather than for long-term health promotional care, but it places nursing in jeopardy of losing the confidence and trust of the public and of the physicians. Nurses themselves will lose faith and confidence in their profession also, as they come to realize that nursing standards of care are no longer valued and are not utilized to promote nurses' allegiance to their profession.

64. ON ANIMAL CONTROL

One of the cases that stands out in my mind over the past three weeks is that of a tall stockily built man living out in Billings. In his sixties, Charlie had a long history of heart attacks and strokes. He had his first heart attack at age 21 years, yet here he was, living alone with his dog in a cold, ramshackle converted summer cottage near a lake. Charlie's personal hygiene is excellent; he says he prepares his own meals, even though he cannot use one arm and hand, and seems both courageous and stoical about his life. A laboratory technician comes each week to draw his prothrombin time. However, the conditions under which I worked that day were horrendous and unforgettable.

Charlie was the eighth patient whom I visited. He lives at the top of a steep icy narrow dirt road with no place for me to park my car. I finally parked in someone else's space and made my way through the ice and deep snow to the chain-link fence and gate. I could not open the gate. Charlie's large black dog, who was thankfully confined inside the fence, was barking and snarling furiously at me. Charlie finally came outside and told the dog to quiet down. Instead, the dog proceeded to jump all over me. Charlie restrained the dog and I finally got inside the house, but still the dog would not lie down. He kept nudging and jumping up on me the entire length of my visit. Fortunately, he was not vicious. I doubt that any homemaker would agree to work in that house. I certainly would never agree to visit Charlie again, unless the dog was tied up and summer weather made the roadway more passable.

65. ESCALATING COSTS OF MEDICARE BENEFITS

Another patient, a 93 year old lady, was confined to a geriatric chair in front of a bow window in her daughter's meticulously clean home. Letitia has a very severe cardiac condition with advanced congestive heart failure and poor circulation in her feet. Her toes are cold and blue, small areas of dry gangrene are present on her feet and in the corners of her nail beds. Letitia's lungs are half-filled with fluid and she is on oxygen continuously at 3 liters. She is given massive doses of diuretic and potassium each day, as well as all the other drugs which stimulate and regulate the cardio-pulmonary system, in an effort to prolong her life. The daughter employs an eight hour a day home health aide privately, and together they are doing an excellent job of keeping mother alive and comfortable. The daughter, who is over sixty years, can no longer lift her mother. She was able to have Medicare pay for a Hoya lift to transfer Letitia from bed to chair and vice-versa. There is also an electric hospital bed which the daughter paid for herself. I suppose this type of equipment will become the norm over the next several years, as more and more frail elders in their nineties are cared for at home by sons and daughters in their sixties and seventies. It's very expensive equipment; I wonder how Medicare will be able to pay for it all.

66. EFFECTS OF MANAGED CARE ON THE MENTALLY ILL

One day, returning to work in a very poor section of the city, I visited a young woman in her 40's, who is unable to be employed because of severe bipolar, or manic depression. Although initially shy and withdrawn, she soon began to share her concerns with me. I seem to have an ability to relate easily to patients with mental illness; they enjoy talking with me and appear to trust me readily. This woman has a history of life-long high blood pressure, as do other members of her family; and as she is on Lithium, she must be monitored frequently. Until recently, she was regularly seen at a community mental health center, and had her own physician there. With the abrupt change-over to managed care by Medicaid in this state, all of the mentally ill persons are being reassigned to new health care providers. In the interim visiting nurses have been asked to provide some continuity of care, so that the patients will not feel so abandoned. Unfortunately, this woman and many others are visited by temporary contract nurses, as there are not enough primary nurses, so not much continuity of care ensues, nor are contract nurses necessarily experienced in mental health nursing care. These patients are the ones who most need the consistent care and concern of primary nurses, but they rarely receive this benefit. With the present budgetary constraints, I wonder if these young persons will ever again receive consistent, comprehensive, supervised health care which they need to remain stable and fairly independent in the community.

67. POSITIVE EFFECTS OF A STABLE LIFE-STYLE

One patient in a large apartment complex in Lee stands out in my mind as having an unusual medical history. I have visited her several times, as she has a monthly Vitamin B12 injection, and needs frequent assessment of her cardiac condition. Janet is now 86 years old, a small-boned seemingly frail widow whose five of six adult children have predeceased her. Volunteers escort her to a community center three times a week to play bingo and grandchildren visit her often. Janet's medical problems include pernicious anemia, atrial fibrillation, severe arthritis, C.O.P.D. (chronic obstructive pulmonary disease), and asthma. She weighs less than 100 pounds. Janet informed me, much to my amazement, that she had weighed only two pounds at birth, and was nursed through a precarious childhood by her father, who was a Canadian Indian medicine man. He knew the herbal remedies which helped her to survive all of the childhood infectious diseases, including whooping cough. Here she is, alive and fairly well, living alone in a neat, clean apartment, able to prepare light meals and to take care of her own personal hygiene needs. I found her to be quite remarkable, both in her ability to survive and in her cheerful, accepting attitude about life.

68. NEGATIVE EFFECTS OF LIFELONG SMOKING

An older man living out in Downey with his wife of many years, also caught my attention. Bill has severe C.O.P.D., can ambulate only a few steps due to shortness of breath, and spends much of his time at the kitchen table in a wheelchair. He self-administers four different inhalers, carefully timed, several times a day. The entire medication process takes at least one-half hour each time. Each one of the inhalant agents must be taken in the correct order to facilitate bronchial dilatation and expansion for adequate air exchange. He holds a stop watch in one hand, and administers the inhalant with the other. Bill informed me that he had been a steel worker and a smoker. Back in the '40's, he said, no one knew about the adverse effects of cigarette smoking. His wife seems to think that he is going to get much better on his new medication regime, but I am afraid they both have unrealistic expectations of his future quality of life.

Julia Stevens, RN, MSN

69. FUTILE VERSUS WORTHWHILE DIALYSIS CARE

February 2, 1993. I saw six patients today, all within the city of Lee. The first was to a man who lived with his wife in a large apartment complex. He was undergoing renal dialysis three times a week. Today he was having difficulty breathing, and had taken two Nitro before my arrival. I realized shortly that this was a very futile case, for he was smoking, his wife smoked, and when his daughter arrived, she too lit a cigarette. I was exasperated. This man already had had an amputation of one leg, had a non-healing, draining decubitus ulcer on his coccyx, and his other leg and foot are swollen, dusky-blue and cold. His lungs had some rales, and he coughed occasionally. I had difficulty feeling much empathy for him, especially when I tried to discuss the advantages of cigarette cessation, but to no avail. I changed the dressing on his coccyx, and explained to his wife the necessity of changing the dressing daily, using clean technique. She seemed to understand, and I moved on to the next case, not feeling very well after inhaling so much smoke.

The next woman I saw was a tall, quiet, dignified person in her seventies, an African-American, who self-administered her own peritoneal dialysis four times each day. Her blood pressure was frequently elevated, and she had little use of her right arm, following a stroke. She was fortunate in having two home health aides, who worked alternate days seven days a week.

They did meal preparation and clean-up, assisted the patient with personal care, did the laundry, and helped set up the dialysis bags and other equipment. I felt that our health care dollars were well-spent on this lady, whose quality of life is very good with this consistent, well-organized care system in place.

70. CREATING DOCUMENTATION FOR MEDICARE REIMBURSEMENT

Another visit that week was to a 64 year old emaciated man living on the second floor of an old three decker house which had been converted to small three room apartments. He had an amputation of his right foot and lower leg and is bitter about this. He has inoperable cancer of the lung, but still smokes a pack or two a day. He is also a severe alcoholic with no intention of desisting—he told me he consumes five bottles of beer every day. He is fortunate in having a homemaker who comes in every day to cook, clean and shop for him. She even helps him bathe. I wondered why we were involved in his care. He is not on any medications and he refuses to renew his multivitamin prescription. I couldn't find anything positive to do there that would qualify this visit for Medicare reimbursement, other than my physical assessment. Thus I had to document such ordinary things as "skin intact and hydrated", "patient not in pain", "teaching to instruct patient on need to renew multivitamins and to eat adequate amounts of protein, carbohydrates and fats", knowing that the patient had no intention of following through. I felt this visit was a complete waste of Medicare dollars and that I had been coerced into creating documentation that was inconsequential. As a taxpayer, it made me feel angry. Possibly, the supervisor would discharge this patient promptly when she read my report or refer him to another type of agency.

71. MORE EFFECTS OF SMOKING, REVISITED

The fourth patient I saw today was about 66 years old, obese, and who lived alone on the first floor of her home. Her daughter-in-law was present and was smoking. The patient's own daughter who was also present, a nurse and quite obese herself, lived upstairs and is a heavy smoker. The patient, who had had a stroke, has a foley catheter and is currently being treated for lung cancer, fluid retention, a stubborn vaginal infection and constipation. She is unable to care for herself, appearing to have memory loss. I became quite perturbed while conducting the patient's assessment, for my nose began to drip and my eyes to water and I began to cough. I realized that this must be due to the smoke in the room, so I hurried through my tasks, not doing as thorough a job as usual, and left as soon as possible. I instinctively knew that I could not ask the daughter-in-law to stop smoking; for I sensed she would become hostile and defensive and my request would probably make the next nurse's visit quite unpleasant.

72. EFFECTS OF INSURANCE REQUIREMENTS ON HEALING

The next patient lived just down the street on the first floor of a spacious apartment building. Beatrice was a woman of sixtyish years who had had an emergency colostomy for a ruptured colon due to diverticulitis. She had been a smoker but had ceased since her surgery. There were still cigarette stubs in an ashtray and the rooms smelled of stale smoke. I was there to do a dressing change on her incision which had not healed properly and also to teach her colostomy care. Beatrice was having difficulty concentrating on learning the technique. She was quite anxious about possibly losing her job, due to her prolonged recovery. She works in a school cafeteria and has health insurance through the city. But in order to have our visits covered and to ensure her job continuance, she had to quickly arrange to present herself to the city physician, her surgeon and her primary physician in order to sign affidavits. This seemed ridiculous to me in view of her diagnosis, treatment and complications thereof. Beatrice mentioned a son who was trying to arrange a day's leave from his job so he could escort her on her mandatory rounds of the physicians. I hoped she would have the endurance necessary for this arduous task, which had to be accomplished all in one day's time.

73. THE SATISFACTION OF BURN DRESSING CARE

The next week I was assigned to a patient way out in Tisbury. It took me a good half hour to find my way there. This young married man required both an early morning and a late afternoon visit to change the dressings on his hands which had been badly burned in a grease fire in his kitchen. The initial pain was so severe that he had also fallen and fractured his foot. Thus he was quite incapacitated and expressed his feelings of frustration and boredom, as well as his anxiety that his insurance company would not cover the full cost of nursing visits.

We determined that the cost of nursing visits was far, far less than visits to the hospital outpatient department would be and that he could apply to the VNA for a reduced fee based on ability to pay. I then happily proceeded to utilize my sterile dressing procedure skills in gently removing the soiled dressings, cleansing and treating the burns and then recovering his tender hands with new sterile dressings. I say "happily" because sterile dressing changes incorporate a set of skills which are easily completed when the home environment is satisfactory, and give the nurse a fine sense of accomplishment. In this case, there was a clean kitchen table, adequate dressing supplies, sterile gloves, and a cooperative patient. I reviewed again with him the need for daily temperature taking, additional protein foods and vitamin A, C and E supplements to promote prompt wound healing, but I couldn't help him very much with his boredom.

74. WHEN THERE ARE NO RECORDS, EXPECT SURPRISES

That was the beginning of a very difficult day, as I had no patient records with me with which to confirm places of residence, diagnoses, treatment plans, or physicians' phone numbers. During the course of the winter, the unavailability of patient records occured repeatedly as primary nurses fell sick with their patient records in their possession, or weekend nurses failed to return patient records before I left the office to make my rounds. This factor gave me a heightened sense of insecurity and anxiety, unless I had seen the patient previously, for I couldn't be sure that I was following the most up-to date care plan, or that the medications on the patient's table or shelf were the correct ones. We did have the previous nurses' pink report forms in each home, but they usually were of no help, for the printing was too faded to interpret clearly.

My next visit was to an elderly lady in Lee who lived in a stately Victorian style home with her son and brother. Ellen appears to be suffering from a severe memory deficit, which may be Alzheimer's. Ellen's beautifully decorated bedroom was on the second floor, with a nearby bathroom just off the elegant upstairs hall. I was there ostensibly to orient a new home health aide to the patient's care, but came upon quite a number of problems. In the first place, the home health aide did not arrive as scheduled, and as I had eight patients to see that day, I was becoming more and more upset with the time lost. I then discovered that this lady had an incision on her left leg, closed with staples, which extended all the way from her foot to her groin, but no incision on her chest. I assumed she had had a femoral by-pass operation of some sort. The patient could not relate anything to me and her brother, who talked and talked, but gave me no real information, also did not seem capable of his sister's care. That is, he didn't seem able to carry out my directions nor to understand the need for handing his sister a glass of fluid every hour. I guessed that the other brother, who was an employed teacher, must run the household.

75. COMMUNICATING EFFECTIVELY WITH ALZHEIMER'S PATIENTS

I visited Ellen several times during the next two weeks. She has diabetes mellitus, diet controlled, a circulatory disorder of her legs and feet, a history of cancer of the breast with mastectomy, and a stroke. Ellen can only walk with assistance, and must have a one-step directional order for any activity at all, otherwise she just sits and naps in her chair. She can be quite stubborn, especially if presented with more than one choice or with a new caretaker. She responds cooperatively when treated with utmost courtesy and respect and informed in a calm voice in simple terms as to what is going to happen next. I tried hard to impart these basic communication techniques to a number of home health aides whom I oriented there. Some understood and developed a fine working rapport with the patient. Others did not, remaining on this case only one or two days. Then I would be asked to orient still another home health aide.

76. ON RESISTANT FAMILIES

Over the course of several weeks, I visited Ellen many times. She developed a red, hot, swollen left foot and leg in the area of her incision, which looked like cellulitis to me. I spent considerable time that day arranging by telephone for her to be taken into Boston to see her surgeon. Her family was not eager to undertake this journey, due to the weather and the son's teaching responsibilities, and tried to have me arrange a visit with her local primary physician. Resistant families present additional problems for the contract nurse, as she doesn't know the family's background and usual behavioral response, and the family doesn't always trust her judgement.

77. RECURRENT INFECTIONS IN DIABETIC PATIENTS

Ellen next developed an infection in the small incision in her abdomen. It's location under the large fatty fold of her stomach made care and healing of the wound difficult. The incision exuded thick malodorous green drainage; the incision had to be thoroughly cleansed, antibiotic applied and a clean sterile dressing applied at least once daily for many, many weeks. Assisting Ellen to move from her chair into a prone position on her bed or sofa for the dressing procedure occupied at least ten minutes of my precious time, for I had to be very gentle, patient and calm with this lady, giving her soothing encouragement every step of the way. Another time Ellen developed a middle ear infection; I noticed that she seemed in pain one day, was running a slight fever, and said she didn't feel well. I noted that her neck glands were swollen and that she was holding her right ear. I asked her brother to give her a Tylenol, extra fluids, and to make an appointment with her primary physician that very day, which he apparently did accomplish, for the next time I visited, she was feeling fine.

78. VISITING THE ACUTELY ILL IN RURAL DISTRICTS

I've now been in Lee several months, and this week has been extremely stressful and busy. I realize now how important it is that I record my observations and events of the day immediately on my return home, for verbally recording the day's events helps to relieve me of great stress and fatigue. This past week I was again assigned to Billings, the rural town I least like to visit. I had six patients to see, at far corners of the town, and an admission case to be completed. It took me an hour to find the new admission's home, and I spent about an hour and half in the home, reviewing the patient's medications, explaining and having her sign all the admission papers, and generally getting acquainted and ascertaining her problems and home care needs. This year the admission papers include several documents pertaining to the living will concept, which often are difficult for patients to comprehend, requiring more precious time on the nurse's part to explain and obtain their signatures.

Another patient I went to see lived alone near a lake in a small converted summer cottage on a lonely dirt road. Elvira was slowly dying of multiple myeloma, was in considerable pain and having difficulty breathing. I noted that her lungs were filling up with fluid, and her ankles were swollen. I called her physician, leaving the facts of the patient's condition with his office nurse, who said that he would undoubtedly recommend hospitalization. I reiterated this information to the patient, who seemed relieved that she would be returning to the hospital for relief of her symptoms. Thank heavens for compassionate physicians!

Eventually I found the other patients' homes, then was delayed in a traffic tie-up, and didn't return to the office until very late in the afternoon. It was too late to complete the admission process there, so I took that folder home and worked on it for one and a half hours that evening after supper. Now I don't mind occasionally doing paper work at home, but I do mind not being paid for this extra effort, since it would not have been necessary had I been assigned to a more familiar area with adequate driving directions to people's homes.

The next day I called my agent, and was informed that indeed I should be reimbursed for completing an admission at home. They told me how to proceed, and I was eventually reimbursed, although I sensed a reluctance on the supervisor's part to sign the necessary form. I felt much better, but still had the nagging feeling that the supervisor might think I was either just inefficient, or trying to obtain extra pay without real justification. This seems to be a growing problem for me and other contract nurses, who are assigned increasingly ill patients who live in out-of-the-way places, and who have difficulty understanding and agreeing to sign the complex admission papers, thus prolonging the length of the home visit.

79. EFFECTS OF ILL-PLANNED HOSPITAL DISCHARGE

The next day in Lee I saw a number of quite sick people and admitted a woman who had just been discharged from hospital and is now on thrice weekly renal dialysis treatments. This 60 year old rather stout and very pleasant patient was having great difficulty getting around her house and caring for herself. Her left arm was unusable as the surgeons had made four incisions in the arm in an effort to place a viable dialysis shunt. The arm was sore and tender, but not infected. Her girth made personal care nearly impossible, and she was somewhat unstable on her feet. She had numerous medications, all of which had to be carefully explained to her and I had to feel assured that she knew how to take them correctly. By the time I had explained all of the admission paperwork, obtained her signatures, and given her peri care, as she couldn't bathe herself, a couple of hours had gone by. The hospital's discharge staff had not arranged for a home health aide or housekeeper, perhaps because the patient was underage for Medicare. I assured the patient that a home health aide would be assigned as soon as possible to assist her with personal care and meal preparation.

The next work day was Friday, and an easier day for me. The two most memorable cases included the woman I had admitted two days ago who was on dialysis. I had to give her an injection of a new drug for boosting the patient's immune status, help her with her medications, and give her a sponge bath and peri care, as there was no health aide assigned as yet. I found out later that I should have filled out a special pink form in the office on this patient's admission day. I did that today upon my return to the office, but was dismayed to find that this process took another half an hour of unpaid time. This was just another example of a contract nurse being utilized inappropriately—admissions should always be conducted by regular primary staff nurses, for they have been instructed in all of the necessary procedures and are paid for all of their time spent on the patient's behalf.

80. EFFECTS OF CHRONIC CONSTIPATION

The other case today that I shall never forget was to a French-speaking elderly woman who lived with a daughter-in-law in a one-story ranch home heated entirely by wood, off a dirt road. There were no directions to her home and no house numbers on the houses, so it took me awhile to find her. The supervisor who asked me to see this woman had been apologetic, saying that the regular primary nurse couldn't handle this case any more. I soon discovered why this was the case. The patient was totally impacted with feces; I have never in my long life as a nurse, seen such impaction. I gave her an oil retention enema which didn't really work as she wouldn't lie down and hold it in for a long enough period of time. I escorted her to the bathroom and the stool finally did begin to come out; I was able to manually disimpact her alternately with the oil enema over the course of an hour and a half while she was seated on the toilet. I discussed the need for prune juice, metamucil, cereals, and much water but knew these measures would be of little help, for she had little muscle tone in her rectum and was unable to bear down to defecate. I suspect that this poor woman had suffered from constipation all of her life and had further complicated the situation by using laxatives that gradually destroyed the normal muscle tone of her colon and rectum. I expect that the VNA is in for a long winter of giving this woman an enema every ten days or so. My back felt nearly broken from the lengthy effort of leaning over the woman seated on the toilet in order to perform the procedure. I won't agree to visit this woman again, as it's too physically stressful.

I am feeling awfully tired these days. I don't know whether it's due to the cold weather, the stress of caring for a different group of acutely ill patients every day, or if perhaps I'm becoming bored with this type of nursing. Perhaps I'm beginning to feel too isolated from the main body of community health nurses. It is probably time for me to seek another staff position, one that would enable me to share my knowledge and increase my administrative skills. The problem is that then I would not have the most interesting challenge of direct patient care and would have to work inside an office every day. Community health agencies have no "clinical ladders" to climb; one has to be either a staff primary nurse or a supervisor.

81. ANOTHER HORRENDOUS SITUATION

I want to add a postscript to my work of this past week—a case I saw on Wednesday, which apparently affected me very much—so much so that I haven't been able to put it into words until now. The patient and his wife were temporarily living in a large renovated white apartment house in a section of the city with which I was not familiar. It took me quite awhile to find the building and then to locate the correct entrance door. Then I walked upstairs and down a long corridor looking for the numbered door. I knocked and waited for several minutes. When I got inside, I was immediately engulfed in hot air—the room was stiflingly hot, at least 90 degrees F. I took off my coat, boots and sweater, but I couldn't doff my wool-lined slacks or the warm tights worn next to my skin for extra warmth in winter. I soon became exceedingly uncomfortable. The wife explained that they had no control over their heat. The patient was sitting up in a chair because he was too weak to walk over to his bed. He was a large, tall man dying of cancer of the mouth, metastized. He was grotesque in appearance, with his mouth hanging open and his swollen tongue protruding. He couldn't speak, but his expressive eyes told me immediately of his great discomfort and despair. His face was misshapened; his feet and ankles swollen. I was absolutely horrified to see a human being in such distress. When I touched his forehead I immediately knew he was feverish and probably dehydrated. He seemed to be in pain, also. I took his temperature under his armpit, and found it to be 100 degrees F. I asked his wife to crush two extra-strength Tylenol and administered these with water through the G-tube into his stomach. Within ten minutes the patient appeared to be more comfortable. I noted a foul greenish discharge from his mouth, and knew there was infection present. He had not voided since last night.

This couple are Medicaid recipients and have moved from place to place frequently. They have no regular physician, but were last seen two days ago in the oncology clinic of the city hospital. I finally located the physician there by telephone; he was most kind and understanding, but didn't want to admit the patient to the hospital yet. He asked me to arrange for Hospice services in the home. I called the VNA and spoke with the supervisor who said that the admitting process for Hospice would soon be underway, and for me to inform the couple that a hospice team would arrive in a day or so. I said that the couple was in dire straits, and needed a hospital bed and home health aide assistance right away, that two days hence would be too late. I reviewed the patient's medications with the wife, who seemed to be trying hard to care for her husband, for the apartment was neat and clean. She was; however, very small in stature and unable to either lift him or assist him safely in walking. I considered trying to assist him to his bed with her help, but realized that there was too great a risk of his falling down. I left there feeling very frustrated and sad that it would take so long to make this dying man comfortable. I wasn't able to sleep well that night, as visions of that poor man floated before my eyes. He and his wife seemed to have been abandoned by the community.

I have since learned from staff nurses that the patient with the advanced cancer of the tongue had been admitted to the hospital shortly after my visit, where he died a merciful death. I felt relief that he was no longer suffering, and that my initial assessment had been correct—he needed to be in the hospital receiving pain killers and comfort care for the terminally ill—not left sitting up in a stifling room with his tiny wife trying to administer to his overwhelming needs all by herself. I wonder what different information was given the physician by the hospice team which prompted him to readmit the patient. Possibly this physician had worked with the hospice team previously and trusted their judgment over mine.

82. ADMIRATION FOR SPOUSAL CARE

I have been all over Lee, Downey and Tisbury in the past two weeks. One case that stands out in my mind is that of a couple in their late sixties living in a condominium in Tisbury. The wife had had a mastectomy several weeks ago; unfortunately the incision line had become infected. A tunnel had formed under the incision, running all the way across her chest from the outer rib cage to her sternum. A huge amount of gunky, prurulent sero-sanguinous drainage was pouring out of the opening in the outer wall. The physician had ordered the nurses to irrigate the wound three times a day with a solution of half hydrogen peroxide, half water, to be followed by insertion of a 3 by 3 gauze, twisted to form a wick, all the way inside the tunnel to the sternum, a distance of six to eight inches. However, the couple's insurance would only pay for one visit per day of a registered nurse. I ascertained that the husband had a fairly good grasp of clean technique and of universal wound precautions, but I was astounded that he was willing to perform such a gory, unpleasant task on his wife. On my next visit, he conducted the entire procedure in a very matter-of-fact and competent manner. His wife didn't seem to mind, either. I realized I had learned another lesson in husbands' ability to transcend the intimate nature of complex mastectomy care in order to help bring about rapid healing without hospitalization.

83. EFFICACY OF PERFORMING BASIC NURSING CARE

February 1993. I saw eight patients today living in a large district of some 20 miles in area. I first visited a frail bed-bound elderly woman with severe atelectasis. She lived with her husband, who has cancer, in a lovely large old colonial home. Her hospital bed was set up in the middle of the front parlor. I noted a baby's crib in one corner. This very ill woman was having great difficulty breathing and in coughing up phlegm. I could hear phlegm rattling way down in her throat. She was all crumpled up in the bed and was complaining of great fatigue and inability to get any rest because of constant coughing. I asked if I could pull her up in bed and rearrange her pillows, and she gratefully acceeded. I proceeded to lower the head of the bed, pull her way up, elevate the head of the bed, and then arrange her pillows in the V fashion I had been taught nearly forty years ago in nursing school. She was astounded with the immediate comfort she felt and the ease with which she could expell phlegm. Ascertaining that she was feverish, I gave her an acetaminophen, administered cough syrup, and persuaded her to drink a cup of hot tea, for she seemed dehydrated. Then I changed her colostomy dressing and emptied her appliance, changed her G-tube dressing, and talked with her about the importance of asking her home health aide to bathe her feet daily and apply lots of lotion, for her legs and feet were in great danger of skin break-down. A year ago I would have bathed her feet myself, but I have now learned that this takes too much of my time and energy and is not an expectation of a contract nurse. Finally, I made up a list of warm fluids that she could tolerate, and then she drifted off into a sound sleep. I was pleased, that in just an hour's time I had been able to make her so much more comfortable.

84. EFFICACIOUS HOSPICE CARE

Next, I traveled to a single-family one story home in which a terminally ill man in his early 50's resided with his wife, college involved daughter, another married son, daughter-in-law and young four year old granddaughter. The latter family had returned from Florida to help care for their father, who has adenocarcinoma and is undergoing chemotherapy and radiation. I was there to substitute for the family's usual Hospice nurse. The household seemed very loving and caring but disorganized, with clothing, shoes, and books strewn all over the floors; very messy indeed.

However, I soon realized that the patient's wife had all she could do to care for her totally incapacitated husband, cook the meals for this large family and mind her little granddaughter. The patient is frequently confused and disoriented. He had climbed out of his hospital bed last night, over the guard rails, and had fallen to the floor, bruising himself in several places. His wife and other members of the family were extremely upset by this, particularly as they all were sleeping in the same room with him, but had not heard him moving about. They felt that he was abusing their care of him. They don't really understand the severity of his mental problems—I presume he has metastasis to the brain, but I could not mention this, of course. He is completely unresponsive to my questions today. The man's skin was in superb condition; he has a home health aide daily for four hours Monday through Friday. She transfers him to a chair, bathes him, does his laundry, helps feed him, and generally lends assistance and support to his wife. I reviewed all his medications with the family, and they are giving them appropriately and understand the purpose and possible side effects. The man is eating well; he has one eschar on his right heel which is firmly in place and non-draining. I suggested that they use sheepskin booties on both feet to further protect them from pressure of the mattress. His lungs were clear; he is recovering from a urinary tract infection and possible pneumonia, and is on an antibiotic. I left that home feeling that everything possible was being done to both keep the patient comfortable and free of complications and to support and assist the family through their terrible ordeal.

85. ON SPOUSAL DEVOTION

I then traveled to the east side of town, a distance of about eight miles, to see a tiny Italian lady with stage three Alzheimer's. Ida was clean and neat and had obviously been a very charming woman before onset of this terrible disorder which now made her speech incoherent. Her husband was taking excellent care of Ida and the house was spotlessly clean. He said he was having trouble getting her to eat adequately, but I found that her weight had not changed. Ida had a little edema in her ankles, but in general seemed to be in good shape. Her skin was intact and smooth; her home health aide was doing a good job with personal hygiene. In response to his mild complaint, I did suggest that the husband could lessen his feelings of confinement by having his wife attend the local adult day health center, where several of the attendees have dementia problems, but he was not ready to accept this idea. I find it somewhat disturbing to see how extremely loyal husbands are to their wives who have Alzheimer's and vice-versa. It's very difficult for them to accept help from others—they don't believe they will suffer burn-out, and I suppose some of them may never, but they certainly do sacrifice themselves completely to care for their spouses.

By four o'clock I had returned to the office and congratulated myself on having seen eight patients in a district where the travel was extensive and the problems varied, but not as horrendous as on some other days. These eight patients all had primary nurses; there was continuity of care, good organization, and viable nursing care plans. I actually felt satisfied with my day's work. I once again noted the vast difference between trying to be a make-shift primary nurse when there is no primary nurse, with the correct role of a contract nurse; that is, of a substitute task oriented nurse for that day only.

86. EFFECTS OF MULTIPLE SNOWSTORMS

It is now the last day of March; I have been on vacation for about ten days. Prior to that time, I had experienced some very difficult and dangerous driving conditions. We had had so many snowstorms of such great depth that one could not see around the street corners to ascertain the presence of on-coming vehicles. It was also very icy underfoot. I managed not to have any accidents, but one nurse did fall and break her leg.

87. EFFORTS TO CARE FOR THE HOMELESS, MENTALLY ILL

I want to describe a situation which is apparently going to reoccur often during the next several months, for the state supreme court has ruled that the state mental health department does not have a responsibility to supervise and care for the homeless mentally ill. One day when I arrived at work, my new supervisor asked me to see seven patients, one of whom was a recently hospital-discharged mentally ill person. When I went to the address given, which was a four decker rooming house, I made several inquiries of the occupants, but no one knew where the patient had moved. I reported this to the supervisor, of course not getting any pay for the hour's time involved. On the next working day, she had located the new address of this man, but he had no telephone, and so I had to simply stop by and hope that he would be there. I knew from experience that this is not a prudent procedure to follow, especially for the mentally ill, who often go outside to shop or just to walk around the city.

I found that David now lived in a boarding home of some sixteen rooms run by a stout and pleasant male supervisor. There were also two elderly ladies, the land-ladies, who lived on the first floor. David has very severe schizophrenia of the manic type. He had just been discharged from a private Boston psychiatric hospital after assaulting one of his land-ladies. The landlady, Anna, told me that she had been attacked with a hatchet by David, and had had eight stitches in her head. Anna had nearly recovered by now and surprisingly was not angry with David; she did not intend to press charges. David was returning to his usual residence of the city of Lee. The supervisor escorted me up to the third floor, back hall, where I was introduced to him.

David is a large, obese male in his early forties who also suffers from seizures and hypertension. He speaks only in the third person; he very adamantly refused my assistance in helping to understand his medications and to take them correctly. David has a rather low I.Q., has been mentally ill most of his life; and had been diagnosed with a learning disability as a child. No family member would take responsibility for him any more. He had been discharged on multiple medications to control his anxiety and his anger and hopefully to prevent hallucinations and seizures.

When David met me at his bedroom door, he was obviously agitated and said: "He don't need me, he has doctor to go to, no nurses, no nurses". I reported to my supervisor that I was unable to admit him but felt that he needed care very soon to prevent further aggression. The next time I worked she sent me back again with an appointment for four o'clock to meet with David and his case-aid worker, with whom he has a trusting relationship. He refused to allow me to take his blood-pressure and was totally confused as to taking his many medications correctly; he had thrown most of them out in the trash barrel, and was becoming more agitated by the hour. We rescued most of the pill containers from the rubbish barrel just outside the front door. I got out my supply of brown pill envelopes and proceeded to fill them with the correct dosages. I labeled them with time of day, the contents, and the day of the week, for the three weekend days that were coming up. The supervisor and land-ladies said they would remind David and assist him with the envelopes. I found out later that this system worked beautifully over that three day period, for David resumed stability and no aggressiveness was noted by the supervisor there. However, I still had not been able to formally admit David to our services, so there could be no pay for me. I reported to my supervisor that she should send a nurse back on the fourth day to admit David and to refill his envelopes, but she did not follow through with this expectation.

When I next worked, on the following Wednesday, I was sent back to see David. The land-lady said that David had refused to see his doctor that morning, and so had not obtained his weekly anti-psychotic injection, that he was all out of pills, and was very agitated. I don't know how she knew all this, but she did. The male supervisor, whom I considered my body-guard, had left for the day. I began to feel very uneasy about ascending those two flights of stairs, and then walking down the back hall to David's room, which was at the very end. I finally decided that I had better not try, for the chances of David's becoming violent upon hearing my voice, were quite great. I felt badly about this, and somewhat angry, for I again could not charge for this third visit. I also felt that my supervisor had inadvertently set me up for failure. On that particular day, David was the ninth patient I saw, or tried to see, so I'm sure my fatigue entered into my temerity. I did see eight patients that day, and the driving conditions were horrendous. I realized to my distress, that my hands were aching when I finally returned to the office. This was new to me, and frightening. I think the combination of driving a gear-shift car with multiple stops for traffic lights, plus the number of visits carrying my heavy nursing bag up and down stairs, caused my arthritis-type discomfort. I decided I needed a rest, and stopped work immediately. I have no idea what happened to David. I know I felt that I had failed, yet I had tried my best. My supervisor was not yet experienced enough to understand the futility of accepting such patients for admission, nor of the inherent risks to the nurse. I suppose I should have refused to try to admit David, but I have always felt a particular empathy for the mentally ill and I am usually successful in making a connection with them.

88. MULTIPLE KNIFE WOUNDS & SEXUAL HARRASSMENT

One day I went to see a memorable Hispanic worker who lived in a high-rise subsidized apartment building in the city. He had suffered several knifing wounds in a street robbery attempt. He had a temporary colostomy, two huge gaping wounds in his belly with sutures to be removed the next day, a supra-pubic catheter which was now out—he was voiding well, and he had a left thigh wound as well. We were packing all of the deep wounds with sterile wet to dry saline dressings, a procedure which took about forty minutes to complete. We had to change sterile gloves several times during these dressing procedures in order to assure that no bacteria would be transferred from one wound to another. However, today the gauze packings all had a greenish tinge stain at the bottom, which caused me some concern, for fear that infection was developing. I wondered if all of the nurses were as careful as I to use sterile technique and glove changes for each wound. He was not on an antibiotic, but had no fever, and no pain. There was no odor either. All during my visit this man flirted with me, and asked questions which could be construed as sexual harassment of me, but I chose to believe that he was trying to be complimentary and dismissed his comments lightly. I documented my wound-care findings carefully for the primary nurse, who would see him the next day.

I moved on to another part of the city where I met a young man in his twenties, who has kidney failure. He performs peritoneal dialysis several times daily and is very competent in this respect, as he soon demonstrated to me. He is awaiting another kidney transplant, the first one having failed. This was a very pleasant and informative visit for me. I am constantly learning about new medical and surgical techniques and treatments which help me to keep up to date with current practices.

Then on to visit another Cambodian family, a grandmother whom I had seen once before. She is still lying on her bed, although it has been many months since I have seen her. Since I knew she had received a long series of physical therapy visits, I had expected her to be up in an armchair or a wheelchair by now. She had had a severe stroke about a year ago, and was paralyzed on her left side. She is still unable to turn, to sit up or to transfer without the assistance of at least one other. There is no cane, no walker or commode to be seen in the apartment, which surprises me. I wondered why this patient was so dependent. I had assisted many persons with at least as severe strokes as this woman's, and they had all made some progress toward semi-independence in a year's time. It is as though she had decided to become a helpless cripple, in order to gain the total attention of her family.

Unfortunately the family members present could not speak or understand enough English for us to have a worthwhile discussion about grandmother's lack of progress. I did discover that she was taking her anti-seizure drug only twice a day rather than the prescribed four times. I think I finally got that essential point across to the family, at least.

The very last patient was an elderly man who lived with his wife in a very attractive converted mill apartment building. He has been having chemotherapy and radiation for terminal cancer, and is holding up quite well. Then I went back to the office and spent the next two hours writing up the admission and doing the rest of my charting in the patients' records. I never did get to do the "486" on one patient because I was becoming so tired that I couldn't concentrate any longer.

I also took in to the clinical director a copy of the journal-manuscript I had written describing my first year's work as an independent contractor, mostly in the city of Lee. I did so with some trepidation, as I wasn't at all sure how they would react to this rather explicit description of actual working conditions in their agency, but I needed to know their impressions and comments before I submitted the manuscript for publication.

89. CARING FOR AN H.I.V.+ PATIENT

I want to describe to you a patient who is HIV positive who made a distinct impression on me. I saw him twice. He lives in a two room apartment on the second floor with only a skylight for a window. Paul is a tall, slender man in his early forties, weighing only 110 pounds, who has just been discharged from the hospital. He is covered from head to toe with the worst case of psoriasis I have ever seen. The dark red wall-to-wall carpeting on his bedroom floor is covered with bits of dry, flaky skin. He is recovering from life-threatening bilateral pneumonia. The physicians had had to perform a tracheotomy in order for him to breathe. I suspect he has full-blown A.I.D.s, but there is no mention of this on his hospital discharge papers. I was there to be sure that Paul was taking his multiple medications correctly and to supervise and possibly teach the home health aide, who never showed up, and to see if he was progressing. Well, he certainly wasn't progressing. Paul was so confused that he could not remember his medication regime at all, and was not taking the pills which would make him more comfortable. For the next half hour, and with his agreement, I proceeded to place his various pills in marked envelopes, as I have described previously, with daily batches secured with elastics, so that he would have less chance of mixing them up. I did not dare prepare more than one week's supply of meds for him, nor did I think it wise to prepare more than twice a day antiinflammatory medication, as he did not have enough food in the house to assure eating before taking the four times a day medication for his joint pain. I did not want him to get into trouble with his G.I. system from the irritating effects of this medication. Paul does seem to have a number of friends, who stop by to see and chat with him and occasionally run errands for him, but they don't do very much about the house. Paul seemed to understand the need to drink fluids and to eat soft foods frequently, but I didn't see how he could walk to the refrigerator to obtain them. I hoped he would enlist his friends to assist him; he said he would.

It was very difficult to move around in his bedroom; the furniture took up all the space. The only table top was the bureau, which was totally covered with all sorts of personal belongings. I spent extra time clearing off and arranging the necessities for his medical care on this surface. Next I assessed and cleaned his tracheotomy, which was badly in need of cleansing and a clean gauze cover and left some supplies for the next nurse, as Paul certainly couldn't do this himself. It was very hard to see this neck wound clearly, as it was a cloudy day and not much sunlight was coming through the skylight. Then I proceeded to don fresh gloves and apply baby oil all over his body, from the top of his head right down to his toes, front and back, to relieve his itching, dry skin and joint distress. His joints were all swollen and hot to the touch. Then I applied a special psoriasis ointment all over his body, after which he said he felt much better. I called the home health aide office at the agency to arrange for another aide for his care. He really needed a full time nursing assistant to care for him, but of course Medicaid would never pay for that level of care. It's doubtful that any home health aide would agree to care for him, for they would be frightened of his appearance and behavior, the condition of his apartment, and the fear of contracting disease themselves. A conference would need to be arranged at the VNA office to discuss Paul's condition and reassure the home health aides as to their safety in caring for him. This could only be accomplished by a primary nurse, and Paul did not yet have one assigned to him.

I saw Paul again a few days later. He stated he had fallen the night before. He is on an anti-AIDs drug, which sometimes causes dizziness and loss of balance. I didn't know just what to do about this. I couldn't reach his physician at that early hour, so finally we agreed that Paul would call and inform his physician about his fall and ask if he should discontinue the medication. Paul stripped again, and I again covered him with baby oil first and then the special psoriasis ointment. He began to look improved, although he said he did not feel much better. I thought perhaps this was a plea for more sympathy and assistance than I could afford to give him. A home health aide had accepted an assignment with Paul for two days a week, two hours at a time. She was preparing a meal for him when I arrived, but stated to me privately that she just couldn't stay on this case. Paul's friends will take him to see his physician this afternoon. I expect they will have to carry him back up the stairs as he is so weak. My back felt nearly broken from leaning over, as his bed was so low to the floor, and I had again spent more than an hour there, in fact, nearly two hours. The outcome for this fairly young man looks quite bleak to me, and makes me feel very sad. I was glad I could relieve his pain a little, and my "laying on of hands" perhaps took away some of his feelings of being an outcast of the community.

90. PLEASURES OF NURSING IN SPRINGTIME

Now I have just returned from a week's vacation. I note from my tape recording that my voice again sounds enthusiastic and is full of cheerful intonations. The snow is all gone, and the driving much easier. I had a very nice day,, seeing seven patients. The first was to a Cambodian grandmother with newly diagnosed diabetes whom I admitted to service. She lives with her multi-generational family in a large, clean two family house in the city. Her son acted as interpreter. She is a small, rather stout woman, pleasant and with a pretty face. I took a fasting capillary blood sugar test with a result of 218 mg. per dL. I discussed the doctor's order for an 1800 calorie A.D.A. (American Diabetic Association) diet and walking exercise with her and her son, trying to adapt this American diet to the typical Cambodian food culture. We settled on rice three times a day, plus lots of vegetables, two servings of fruit, a little fish or chicken, and very little oil in the cooking. I don't know whether this will work, but if not, she can probably take an anti-diabetic pill to control her diabetes. It's difficult in a large three or four generation family; they like to eat together from communal dishes that are prepared by the younger, very hungry family members who need more calories than their grandmother.

Last week was extremely busy at the Lee agency. I saw between six and eight patients each day and had an admission each day as well. I was quite exhausted by the end of the week. The problem is that they don't have enough primary nurses. The care given by the contract nurses is thus necessarily fragmented. It's too bad; I try very hard to act as a primary nurse when I am there, on the basis of one or perhaps two visits, but I am having to spend as much as two hours in some homes in order to ascertain the problems and reach agreement with the families as to a viable plan of action and/or to instruct them in the necessary treatments or drug regimen. As I am paid by the visit on an average time basis of no more than thirty minutes per visit, I am beginning to feel some resentment. However, my innate senses of duty, altruism, and responsibility as well as all of my community/public health education and experience persuade me to complete each visit as thoroughly as possible. I realize that in continuing this practice I am jeopardizing my status as an independent contractor, for discouragement and physical exhaustion will eventually force me to stop this type of nursing.

91. SCHOOL VACATION WEEK BRINGS OUT MULTIPLE STRESSES

The agency seems stressed out this week—I'm sure no one has had time to review my manuscript.. As spring public school vacation occurs next week, many of the primary nurses are attempting to turn their caseloads over to other nurses so that they can have a few days off to be with their own children. The atmosphere in the office feels chaotic—telephones ringing everywhere, nurses using every persuasive technique possible to either reduce the number of visits to each of their patients next week, or discharging them abruptly, or arranging for a per diem nurse to see them. One nurse, who is the mother of three children, looked particularly harassed. She is one of the nurses whom I most admire. She had been a head nurse in a hospital before joining the VNA. I had noted that her work with patients was in the best community health tradition and that she managed her caseload with great skill and efficiency. Unfortunately for the VNA, she stated to me privately that "she had had it and was going to resign"—just "too many patients, and more coming all the time". I sympathized with her, but stated I hoped she would change her mind. Resigning under stress is a common occurence in community health agencies these days. Gone are the days when a nurse managed a reasonable caseload of 20-30 patient-families, most of whom were chronically ill, requiring guidance, counseling and on-going education at a pace which the nurse could control. Maintaining health stability and preventing complications was the goal then. Nowadays, the nurses must deal with acutely ill, post-hospital patients, many of whom have complex diagnoses and highly technological treatments and equipment, needing daily visits and many community resources to be arranged and coordinated. Dealing with the complex details of as many as 45 patients and their anxious families is just too much—nurses become "overloaded" and begin to feel unable to competently manage. Then they begin to fear that they may make an error in judgment, or overlook a significant symptom or drug error, causing patient death or a lawsuit against them. The supervisors or nurse-managers, if they are experienced in community health (and they often are not) can do a lot to alleviate these stressed-out nurses' feelings if they themselves have time to do so. Frequently; however, agencies push supervisors to the limit also, in an effort to secure as many admissions as possible. Competition among agencies for insurance-paying patients is fierce today. According to Stuart-Siddall, in "Home Health Care Nursing" (1986), all of this frantic scurrying has occured since the enactment of Medicare in 1966 and the growth in numbers of proprietary agencies, beginning in 1982 (p. 26-27). Prior to 1966, most home care patients paid in cash or were subsidized through donations to VNAs. Patients remained in hospitals until stabilized or close to becoming well. The primary goal of community health nurses was to maintain or enhance the patient's health and prevent complications from occuring in the chronically ill.

92. ANOTHER COMPLEX ADMISSION

I saw nine patients yesterday. Eight were for routine visits while the other was an admission of a Cambodian man who does not speak English. Fortunately his daughter was there in the clean, second story apartment and she understands and speaks English quite well. My task was to teach, demonstrate and supervise a complete insulin-dependent diabetes regime to this patient, who had just been diagnosed, and who also had been hospitalized with congestive heart failure and a draining heel ulcer. Wet to dry sterile saline dressings had been ordered, so we had to go through the procedure of boiling water on the stove and adding salt. Fortunately, I had brought with me two sterile plastic containers in which to place the sterile solution, and the patient had been discharged with adequate dressing supplies. I had plenty of gloves with me to leave with them so that they could use sterile technique in squeezing the sponge and applying it to the ulcer. As this 55 year old man is blind in one eye, I drew up several syringes with the required 25 units of insulin and noted that he could safely inject himself. I reviewed his diabetic and low sodium dietary requirements with his daughter, trying to adapt our typical diabetic diet to Cambodian foods. I noted that he was also on 40 mg. of diuretic, which seemed excessive to me, as I could not detect any signs of continuing congestive heart failure and he was already so very slender. However, there was no way I could reach his clinic doctors at this early morning hour, and so I noted in the patient's record that assessment for electrolyte imbalance should be undertaken on the nurse's next visit, four days hence. Unfortunately, there was no scale in the house, so we would be unable to determine if he was losing weight too quickly, which could be a indication that a lower dose of diuretic would suffice, and/or that insulin adjustment was needed. There was a time when we nurses routinely carried a scale into patients' homes, but this practice has been discontinued except for premature new-born infants. I gather that the scales disappeared too often. I cared for this man several times over the course of the next three weeks, and was quite pleased with his progress.

93. MY FINALE

It is now May 28, 1993. I have been at home for three weeks' now. I stopped working early in May as I was not feeling well. I was also beginning to suffer "burnout". Because of the primary nurse shortage at the Lee agency, I had been assigned to the same group of patients for several weeks. This was not a serious problem for me with most of the patients, although it was boring, but there was one at least who proved to be my undoing. A thirty year old woman with spina bifida, confined to a wheelchair all of her life, lived with her six year old son in a specially designed apartment for the handicapped in Lee.

Connie had been married, but had lost her husband several years ago. Her major problem at this time was the development of severe draining ulcers on her feet and legs, which were grossly swollen from fluid retention. She now had cellulitis of both legs. We nurses were to change her foot dressings each morning; she was supposed to change them herself each evening. However, she was negligent in doing this, partly because it was so difficult for her to reach her feet. She frequently bumped her feet against walls or furniture, breaking down any beginning healing process, but as she had no feeling in her extremities, this did not bother her at all. Connie suffered from severe headaches, a thyroid disorder, and her blood pressure was frequently elevated. She was having many problems with her current boyfriend. She informed me that she needed to see a gynecologist for menstrual irregularity. I agreed, but found that there was not a single specialist who would see her, as she had only Medicaid insurance. Connie became more and more manipulative as the weeks went by. Sometimes she did not take her meds as ordered, or she decided not to eat. She visited physicians in Boston as well as in Lee, and would often have new prescriptions for her many complaints. The last straw occured after I had been caring for her for about three weeks, making little progress. The most recent primary nurse assigned to Connie's care had refused to make any further visits; thus I cared for her two or three days a week.

One morning, the last time that I saw her, Connie's homemaker had drawn her bathwater for her as usual, but had not felt the temperature. Connie had gotten into a very hot tub of water. When I arrived, the skin on her legs and feet was peeling off in great quantities. She had suffered second degree burns all over both legs and feet. I immediately told her she must call her physician and go to see him quickly. She couldn't locate him by phone. In the meantime I gave her the same care I would any burn patient; that is, applying sterile wet saline dressings over both extremities.

Then I managed to reach her plastic surgeon and made an appointment for her the next day. There seemed no need to send her by ambulance to the emergency room, as she had no pain and was already on an antibiotic. There was no one who could care for her child on such short notice, either. I instructed her not to try to change her dressings herself, and to drink plenty of fluids.

This was another example of a chronically ill person on Medicaid who is not getting coordinated medical care. Connie has too much freedom to see various physicians for her many physical problems, yet cannot obtain needed gynecological care. There is no one physician in charge in whom she has confidence and trust. It's very frustrating trying to care for these disabled persons. They often become very manipulative over their life-spans in an effort to stay alive and have their many needs met.

At this point in time, I decided I had had enough of independent contracting for now. I was acting in the capacity of a primary nurse, but without the back-up support and resources needed to perform optimally. Lack of reimbursement for the extra time spent on each case seemed to indicate that the agency did not really value my work and I certainly no longer felt satisfied with my work. I was truly disappointed in the Lee agency, for I ha believed that this agency's directors were different from others—that they valued their nurses and the optimal conduct of nursing care more than the almighty dollar. I'm sure that there were many factors involved at the management level—Medicare and Medicaid decreases in payment, new and more stringent regulations for recording of care, the advent of managed care constraints, the increased acuity of patients discharged from hospitals, the enormous difficulties in caring for the homeless and mentally ill, and the advent of numerous AIDs and hepatitis patients—all added to the stresses and difficulties of managing this regional visiting nurse, community health care agency.

PART III

SUMMARY & CONCLUSIONS

Julia Stevens, RN, MSN

As I review and compare last year's journal with this year's, I realize how very much more skilled I have become in assessing, treating and evaluating patient care, as well as in predicting outcomes of care. I have been re-reading Patricia Benner's excellent book, "From Novice to Expert" (1984) in which she describes the knowledge and skills advancement from novice nurse to expert clinician. I found many correlations between my personal descriptions of growing skills in assessment, perception, judgment, proficiency, and holistic understanding of the patient-family situation with Benner's description of the five stages of nurse skill acquisition and performance.

I believe that independent contracting will continue to expand in home health care agencies, but I fear for both the quality of patient care and the possible exploitation of the contract nurse. Nurses should be limited to a realistic number of home visits per day to help ensure high quality comprehensive patient care while being compensated more fairly for the actual time spent in each home. Contract nurses' level of education and years of experience should also be acknowledged in their rate of pay. Nursing care agencies need to unite in utilizing identical, non-redundant computerized documentation forms, in providing efficient back-up support and resources for the contract nurse, in designing measurable outcomes for patient care, teaching guidelines and checklists for all medical and surgical diagnoses, and in providing that subtle but imperative model of professional standard-bearing that demonstrates to the contract nurse that her services are valued, and that optimal concern for quality of care is the most important criterion in community health nursing.

In the years to come, as the government moves toward prospective reimbursement for specific population groups, community health clinical nurse specialists can be utilized to plan, direct and promote the health of the chronically ill, such as the frail elderly, diabetics with complex needs, those with severe cardiac and pulmonary disorders, mobility and mental disorders, and premature infants. Block grants or other funding mechanisms which would ensure long-term aggregate group care at the primary and secondary prevention levels could provide an equitable system of high quality care for patient-families and both compensation and professional satisfaction for the independent nurse contractor. Community health nursing agencies could then plan the long-term care of the chronically ill in a cost-effective and judicious manner, no longer having to rely mainly and haphazardly on insurors' per visit payments for episodic care of the acutely ill post-hospitalized individual patient-family.

In addition to the satisfaction of validating in writing my two years' experience as an independent contractor, I have tried to describe the unique working conditions for nurses who visit patient-families in their homes. Such variables as the size of the agency, the number of cities and towns it serves, the presence or absence of experienced supervisors, the acuity of patients recently discharged from community or tertiary-care hospitals, and the amount of documentation required in each agency, all affected my ability to perform home health nursing care. I found that I had to somewhat compromise my standards for total patient care in order to carry out my assignments expeditiously, and I also found that comprehensive case management of the patient-family was impossible to carry out when I managed a caseload of patients when there was no primary nurse. The increasing amount of required documentation for each patient may well take its toll of primary nurses, leaving agencies understaffed and thus unable to meet the demands for nursing care from physicians, hospitals and the community at large.

The completion of this journal has taken me six years—much longer than I anticipated, but affording me additional time for reflection, research and editing to my ultimate satisfaction with this endeavor. This has been a very valuable experience, and one that has shown me how demanding and difficult it is to accurately describe one's personal thoughts, beliefs and behaviors, particularly in regard to other human beings. My own natural empathic attitude was often adversely impacted by environmental conditions, fatigue, or organizational problems at the agency level. However, my excellent nursing education and training served as the basis for making judgments concerning patients' care needs and prioritizing time which surely accomplished some good, and certainly caused no harm. For this, I will always be grateful.

REFERENCES

Benner, P. (1984). <u>From Novice To Expert.</u> Menlo Park, CA: Addison-Wesley Publishing Co.

Community Health Network, Inc. (1989) <u>Requirements for All Accepted Contractors</u> P.O. Box 1658, Cambridge, MA 02238.

Grau, L. (1984). *Case Management and the Nurse.* <u>Geriatric Nursing.</u> Nov./Dec.: (372-375).

Green, J.L. & Driggers, B. (1989). *All Visiting Nurses Are Not Alike: Home Health & Community Health Nursing.* <u>Journal of Community Health Nursing.</u> Vol. 6. (2) (83-93).

Reverby, S. (1987). <u>Ordered To Care The Dilemma of American Nursing. 1850-1945</u> New York, New York. Cambridge University Press.

Stanhope, M. & Lancaster, J. (1988) <u>Community Health Nursing.</u> St. Louis: The C.V. Mosby Company.

Stuart-Siddall. (1986). <u>Home Health Care Nursing.</u> Rockville, MD.: Aspen Systems Corporation.

Toffler, Alvin (1970). <u>Future Shock.</u> New York, New York: Random House.

Zander, K. (1978). <u>Primary Nursing. Theory and Development.</u> Boston: Tufts University Press.

ABOUT THE AUTHOR

The author draws upon twenty-five years of experience in community health agencies, adult day health centers, nursing homes and physician's office nursing. She has also been administrator-supervisor of an official town public health and certified home health agency, and an instructor in community health nursing in a baccalaureate degree program.

The author holds a diploma in nursing from the Massachusetts General Hospital School of Nursing, class of 1954, a B.S.N. degree from Fitchburg State College (1981) and a Master of Science degree in community/public health nursing from Boston University School of Nursing (1987). She has been certified by the American Nurses Association as a clinical specialist in Community/public health nursing and is the author of a guest editorial, *As I See It: Access to Health Care and the Future of Nursing*. Journal of Community Health Nursing. Vol. 4 (2), 65-68. 1987. In 1988, the author was invited to make a poster presentation at the 116th annual meeting of the American Public Health Association of her graduate thesis, *Utilization of Primary Nurses Versus Interim Nurses In Promoting Frail Elders' Stay At Home*, unpublished thesis, Mugar Library, Boston University, 1987.

The author presently serves on the Board of Directors of Community Health & Nursing Services (CHANS) in Brunswick, Maine.

In "Nurse For the Moment" the author describes her two years' experience as an independent contractor making home health visits to 1,027 families, utilizing voice tape recordings with later transcription into a narrative journal format.